8-50

61711

Literacy Challenges
for the more able

a collection of mini projects

Shelagh Moore

Book 3

HOPSCOTCH

EDUCATIONAL PUBLISHING

For Michael Kelliher
Headteacher and School Governor
A gifted and dedicated educator.

Published by
Hopscotch Educational Publishing Ltd
Unit 2
The Old Brushworks
56 Pickwick Road
Corsham
Wiltshire
SN13 9BX

01249 701701

© 2004 Hopscotch Educational Publishing

Written by Shelagh Moore
Series design by Blade Communications
Cover illustration by Sarah Wimperis
Illustrated by Jane Bottomley
Printed by Colorman (Ireland) Ltd

ISBN 1-904307-10-8

Acknowledgments
The author and publisher gratefully acknowledge permission to reproduce copyright material in this book.
'The Dragon and St George' by Michael Foss from *Folk Tales of the British Isles* (Michael O'Mara Books)
Extracts from *Robot Dreams* by Isaac Asimov (Victor Gollancz, 1988)
Extract from *Of Time and Stars* by Sir Arthur C Clarke (Gollancz). Ref Clarke/13/5/03
Extract from ANIMORPHS: THE ILLUSION by K. A. Applegate. Copyright © 1999 by Katherine Applegate. Reprinted by permission of Scholastic Inc. ANIMORPHS is a registered trademark of Scholastic Inc.
Extract from *Mirror Dreams* by Catherine Webb (Time Warner Books UK, 2002)
Extract on 'Philosophy' Reprinted with permission from *Children's Britannica*, © 1997 Encyclopaedia Britannica, Inc.

Every effort has been made to trace the owners of copyright of material in this book and the publisher apologises for any inadvertent omissions. Any persons claiming copyright for any material should contact the publisher who will be happy to pay the permission fees agreed between them and who will amend the information in this book on any subsequent reprint.

Contents

Introduction   4

Challenge 1   **Treasure Island**   5
               Writing a playscript of a modern retelling of Treasure Island

Challenge 2   **Myths and legends**   18
               Writing a report comparing ancient mythical characters with
               modern-day ones

Challenge 3   **Narrative poetry**   34
               Writing a newspaper report based on a story from a classic
               narrative poem

Challenge 4   **Science fiction**   47
               Writing a science fiction story that shows how a scientific
               discovery may be used in the future

Challenge 5   **Fantasy worlds**   67
               Writing a description of a fantasy world and drawing or making
               an accompanying visual representation of it

Challenge 6   **Philosophy**   85
               Exploring questions of ethics and writing a set of agreed rules
               for the class

Challenge 7   **Victorian art and music**   100
               Designing a brochure inviting people to an exhibition of the art
               and music of Victorian times

Challenge 8   **Electrical inventions**   111
               Writing an explanation of how an electrical invention works and
               presenting and explaining a display which shows how this invention
               has made our lives better

Challenge 9   **Adventure playgrounds**   121
               Designing and making a model of an adventure playground for the
               school and giving a presentation to others about it

Challenge 10   **Teeth**   132
               Designing a toothpaste advertisement that will appeal to seven-
               year-olds

Generic sheets   143

Introduction

About the series

Literacy Challenges is a series of four books specifically targeted at the more able child in Key Stages 2 and 3. Each book contains ten challenges or mini projects that the teacher can introduce to the pupils who can then work independently, in pairs or small groups to complete the series of set tasks. Each project encourages the development of time management skills and independent research, culminating in a specific end product, such as a written report, a prepared presentation or a radio programme.

The first five challenges in each book are text-based projects where the pupils are encouraged to explore well-known stories and poems in a variety of different genres. The second five challenges are more cross-curricular projects, designed to develop the pupils' reasoning and cognitive skills.

Each challenge is designed to take three to six weeks if time-tabled on a twice-weekly basis or as part of extra-curricular work for the more able. The challenges do not need to be carried out in any particular order, although each one is matched to the objectives for each term of the *Literacy Framework* and can therefore be carried out in accordance with the required range for each term.

The books are aimed at specific National Curriculum English levels and *Literacy Framework* year groups but the challenges work well with children across the Key Stage 2 and Key Stage 3 age range.

Book 1: English NC levels 2–3; *Literacy Framework* – Year 3
Book 2: English NC levels 3–4; *Literacy Framework* – Year 4
Book 3: English NC levels 4–5; *Literacy Framework* – Year 5
Book 4: English NC levels 5–6; *Literacy Framework* – Year 6

About each book

Each book contains ten challenges that are presented in a specific format – a section of teacher's notes and a collection of photocopiable pages that the teacher can provide for each pupil. (These photocopiable pages are listed in the 'resources required' section of each challenge.)

Teacher's notes
The teacher's notes contain the following information:

Purposes
This outlines the expected learning outcomes for each challenge.

Aims
This defines the aims of each challenge.

Resources required
This lists the resources the teacher needs to provide the pupils with.

The teacher's role
This provides the teacher with all the information she/he needs in order to introduce the challenge to the pupils, plus tips and hints on how to help them when they are using the photocopiable support sheets for each challenge. Links to the National Curriculum and *Literacy Framework* are also provided.

The photocopiable sheets
The photocopiable sheets are intended to be used by the pupils. They could be stapled together (or put into a ring binder) to make a booklet for the pupil (with the 'Challenge sheet' used as a cover page), thereby keeping all the materials together.

'My action planning sheet'
Action planning is an essential part of the challenge. The completion of the challenge may take about three to six weeks if the pupils are given only set times each week for working on their tasks. This sheet provides an opportunity for them to plan their work with definite starts, tasks and deadlines. The teacher needs to ensure that the pupils have planned out the tasks they are carrying out in a manner that is logical and will lead to successful completion of the unit. Completing the sheet immediately after the tasks have been read and discussed allows the pupil and teacher to plan a suitable sequence of work to agreed deadlines. The teacher is also able to plan visits and visitors using this sheet with the pupils.

The teacher's role is to help the pupils understand that action plans often need modification as the work progresses and that this is good practice, not a sign of failure. Pupils who are able to assess their own progress and adapt their planning tend to be those who have more success with completing the set tasks.
Once they have planned their work, the real work (as they will see it) can begin!

The 'Task sheets'
Each challenge is divided into two parts – 'Task sheet 1' and 'Task sheet 2'. 'Task sheet 1' contains a set of activities that prepares the pupil for 'Task sheet 2'. These activities often involve extensive reading, discussion and research. 'Task sheet 2' requires the pupils to use the information gathered in 'Task sheet 1' to write, make or prepare

something, such as an advertising poster, a talk to younger children or a story.

The teacher will need to discuss each stage of the task sheets with the pupils, making sure they understand what they need to do and how they are going to do it. (The 'Planning guidelines sheet' goes into more detail for the pupil).

The task sheets are further supported by additional pupils' sheets (such as text mapping sheets and writing guides) that will enable them to carry out their research and plan and present their work.

The 'Planning guidelines' and 'Resources' sheets

The 'Planning guidelines' provide the pupils with a useful summary of the tasks they have to complete. It includes helpful tips and reminders to help them in their planning.

The 'Resource sheet' provides ideas for research and suggests ways in which the pupils can gather information from a variety of sources. Planning the research and waiting for replies to queries is part of the pupil's action planning. Some tasks will not be easy to complete if speakers and visits are not organised in advance – this is where teacher guidance is important.

IMPORTANT: The teacher will need to ensure the pupils understand that they should not write to, contact or visit a potential source of information without the teacher's consent and guidance.

The 'Mapping' and 'Discussion' sheets and 'Writing guides'

The various mapping and discussion sheets and writing guides enable the pupils to develop their skills in different aspects of speaking and listening, reading and writing. They should be used to help them to understand the structure of the tasks set and how to plan them. They 'map out' the thinking that should go into the planning of the tasks and provide a structured approach to their completion. Teachers and pupils can use the sheets to discuss the tasks and the content that is needed to complete them.

The 'Skills sheets'

The skills sheets enable the able pupil to identify the skills developed and practised while completing the challenges. They are generic documents that cover all the challenges and include subject areas that apply to the various tasks set. The pupil can read the sheets and identify the skills he/she feels that they have demonstrated. The pupil may feel that they have successfully demonstrated the skill or that they need more help with this type of skill. They can use the skills sheet to discuss their progress with their teacher.

Assessment

An assessment sheet has been included for each challenge. It can be used by the teacher to identify the levels and skills achieved. The pupil will know from the assessment, which can be continuous throughout the unit of work, what level they are achieving and what they have still to achieve.

The teacher can use this assessment sheet as part of the pupil's record of work for final level assessments at the end of the academic year.

Organisation

Although the challenges are designed to provide pupils with a self-contained unit of work that they can manage independently, it is essential that the teacher guides them through the whole process and tells them how much time will be allocated to the tasks each week.

Each challenge could form part of a whole class topic with separate work being planned for other pupils in the class. Alternatively it could form part of a regular weekly time slot allocated to the more able pupils in order for them to carry out independent work.

They will, however, need the teacher to guide them through the research work and help them make contact with those who can give them the help they need. The pupils should be encouraged to do their research and make any outside contacts under supervision in school.

Special consideration needs to be given to internet research to ensure that only child-suitable sites are used.

Taking the challenges further

Pupils working on the units may well find that they want to develop a particular aspect of the work that interests them. This should be negotiated with the teacher and put into their planning so that they ensure that they complete the tasks set in the unit as well.

Units can be used to develop aspects of the curriculum that the pupils are studying in more depth and from a different perspective. The cross-curricular approach enables the pupils to see that their literacy skills can be applied effectively in other areas of the curriculum and that there are connections between different subjects that help them to understand them better.

Challenge 1

Treasure Island

Teacher's notes

Purposes

- To investigate how language is used to convey meaning.

- To modernise a pre-twentieth century text without losing the themes and issues contained in it.

- To develop skills of text analysis.

- To develop thinking, planning and time management skills.

Aims

- To read chapters 3 and 4 of Treasure Island by Robert Louis Stevenson and make an incident line of the main events that happen in the story.

- To write a playscript based on a modern retelling of Treasure Island by Robert Louis Stevenson.

Resources required

The pupil will need copies of the following:

1	'Challenge sheet'	page 143
2	'My action planning sheet'	page 144
3	'Task sheets'	pages 10 and 11
4	'Planning guidelines'	page 12
5	'Resources' sheet	page 13
6	'Text map' sheet	page 14
7	'Incident line chart'	page 15
8	'Story update' sheet	page 16
9	'Playscript guide'	page 17
10	'Skills sheets'	page 145–148

Pupils will also need a copy of Treasure Island by Robert Louis Stevenson. A video of the film version would be useful.

The teacher's role

1 Introducing the challenge

Write the following into the top box of a copy of the 'Challenge' sheet (page 143):

> You are going to read chapters 3 and 4 from the book Treasure Island by Robert Louis Stevenson. You are then going to map out the important incidents that happen in these chapters.

> Using this information, you are going to write a playscript to retell these chapters in a modern-day setting.

Then photocopy the 'Challenge sheet' and give it to the pupils. Alternatively, they could be given a blank copy of the sheet and write the challenge on it themselves. It is important for them to have the challenge to refer to.

2 Providing support for the task sheets

Reading the text

Introduce the book to the pupils. Tell them that it was written in 1881 and was first published as a serial for a boys' newspaper. Explain that the story itself was set in the 1700s and tells the story of a boy called Jim who finds a map showing the location of treasure hidden on a remote island and how he goes in search of it.

Before reading the text with the pupils, find out what they already know about the book, the author and life in the 1700s. Give them a summary of the story up to Chapter 3 so that they understand how the captain came to be at the inn. (See below.)

> #### Information about the author and text
>
> R L Stevenson was born in Scotland in 1850 and died on the islands of the South Seas in 1894. He studied engineering and law. He travelled in France and America before settling in Samoa. He wrote Treasure Island in 1881 as a serial for a boys' newspaper.
>
> Treasure Island is about a boy named Jim who acquires a treasure map from a dead pirate and, with Squire Trelawney and Dr Livesay, goes to find the treasure. Chapter 1 introduces us to the story that Jim is telling after his adventures are over. His father kept the Admiral Benbow Inn, which was situated along a quiet part of the coast. A mysterious seaman came to stay there. He was silent and watched the cove at lot and he was worried about seamen visiting the inn. He drank heavily and told fearful stories. He paid Jim to watch for a seafaring man with one leg.
>
> In Chapter 2 we learn that Jim's father is seriously ill. A strange man comes to the inn. The stranger asks after 'Bill' only to be told that the only seafaring man in the inn is the captain. The man waits for his 'friend' Bill with Jim. When the man and Bill meet, we learn that the man is really called 'Black Dog'. They sit and talk at the table but a fight breaks out and Black Dog flees. The captain – Billy Bones as he is

called – becomes ill and the doctor attends him and tells him to rest in his bed and stop drinking rum. The captain is very distressed by Black Dog's visit.

Then read the first two chapters with the pupils. Discuss how the author has used language in the narrative and the dialogue to portray the characters and the setting. Help the pupils to identify words and phrases that seem old-fashioned to us today. Has the language used restricted their understanding in any way? Has it helped to build up images in their minds?

Questions that could be asked include:

- 'What is it about the way the captain speaks that tells the reader about his character? Find examples in the text.'
  - 'Why were Jim and his mother so anxious after the captain died? Find examples in the text that tell us how they were feeling.'
- 'How does Jim convey his feelings to the reader? Give some examples from the text.'
- 'How does the blind man help create the feeling of fear? Give examples from the text.'

The pupils should now read chapters 3 and 4.

Using the 'Text map' sheet
This sheet can be used to help the pupils tease out the storyline as suggested in 'Task sheet 1'. The questions about themes and issues should encourage thought and discussion about ethical issues that arise in the story. The pupils should be encouraged to think about how a modern-day boy might deal with the situations that Jim had to deal with.

Using the 'Incident line chart'
This sheet allows pupils to identify the building blocks of the story and to put them in chronological order. This will help them to order the story when writing the playscript as part of 'Task sheet 2'.

Using the 'Story update' sheet
This sheet helps the pupils to review the setting, characters and incidents of the story in order to change them into a modern-day version for their playscript.

Using the 'Playscript guide'
This sheet enables the pupil to plan and structure the playscript. An important part of the planning is deciding the sort of set that will be used because this will determine the visual effects that can be created. Pupils need reminding that a play is a visual as well as an auditory experience so costumes and lighting need careful

consideration. A decision also needs to be made about who the audience will be because this will greatly influence the language level at which the play is to be written.

Provide samples of playscripts for the pupils to view before they commence their own in order to revise scripting layout and style.

3 Other points to note

As they complete 'Task sheet 1', they should be encouraged to begin thinking about how the story could be given a modern-day setting. How could the incidents be made believable if they happened today? Would the characters be different in any way? How might the reactions of the villagers be different in today's society?

The teacher's role for 'Task sheet 2' is to help the pupils use the information they have gathered from 'Task sheet 1', together with the 'Story update' sheet, to plan out their playscript. Revise the conventions of playscripting with them to make sure they understand how a playscript is presented. (The 'Playscript guide' sheet is also useful here.) The pupils need to be reminded of the importance of dialogue and stage directions in conveying the personality and actions of a character in a play, compared with the narrative tools of a story writer. Encourage them to word-process their playscript, using different fonts and italics as suggested in the playscript guide.

Links to the National Curriculum

English – Speaking and Listening
Level 4: Pupils' talk is adapted to the purpose; developing ideas thoughtfully and conveying their opinions clearly.
Level 5: In discussion …they make contributions that take account of others' views.

English – Reading
Level 4: Pupils show understanding of significant ideas, themes, events and characters.
Level 5: Pupils identify key features, themes and characters in the text.

English – Writing
Level 4: Vocabulary choices are often adventurous and words are used for effect.
Level 5: Writing conveys meaning clearly in the form of a play-script for different readers and audience.

ICT
Level 4: ICT is used to present information in different forms and shows awareness of the intended audience.

Challenge 1 continued

Level 5: ICT is used to present information in different forms and show awareness of the intended audience.
Pictures and plans are used to show the setting of the play.

Design & Technology

Level 4: Pupils produce step-by-step plans. They reflect on their designs as they develop.
Level 5: Pupils clarify their ideas through discussion, drawing and modelling. They work from their own detailed plans. They check their work as it develops and modify their approach in the light of progress.

Links to Literacy Framework

Year 5, Term 1

Word level work
W3 – use dictionaries and IT spell-checks.

Sentence level work
S4 – to adapt texts for different purposes.

Text level work
T5 – to understand dramatic conventions.
T18 – to write own playscript.

Assessment sheet

Name: _____ Date: _____

	Achieved	To achieve

Speaking and Listening:

Level 4:
- Talk is adapted to the purpose: developing ideas thoughtfully.

Level 5:
- Makes contributions that take account of others' views and evaluates ideas expressed.

Reading:

Level 4:
- Shows understanding of significant ideas, themes, events and characters.

Level 5:
- Key features are identified including themes and characters.

Writing:

Level 4:
- Vocabulary choices are often adventurous and words are used for effect.

Level 5:
- Writing conveys meaning clearly in the form of a playscript.

ICT:

Level 4:
- Uses ICT to present information in different forms.

Level 5:
- Uses ICT to structure, refine and present information in different forms and styles for specific audiences.

Design & Technology:

Level 4:
- Produces step-by-step plans.
- Reflects on his/her designs as they develop.

Level 5:
- Clarifies ideas through discussion, drawing and modelling.
- Works from own detailed plans.
- Checks work as it develops and modifies approach in the light of progress.

Task sheet 1

Reading a text

Aim

To read chapters 3 and 4 of *Treasure Island* by Robert Louis Stevenson and make an incident line of the main events that happen in the story.

Tasks

- Use the **My action planning sheet** to help you plan your work.

- **Read** the two chapters through carefully.

- **Map out** the text using the **Text map sheet**. Think about the plot, the characters and the issues that the reader is told about by the author.

- **Discuss the story** with someone in your group. What are the important things that happen that make the story interesting?

- **Make a list** of what happens in Chapters 3 and 4 in the order they occur in the story. Use the **Incident line sheet** to help you.

- Now **think** about how you might retell the story if it were to happen today. Think about:

  – the setting: how might this be different today?

  – the characters: what sort of people might they be today?

  – what happens: how could you make the story believable if it happened today?

- **Discuss** your ideas with someone else and **make a note** of any ideas you have.

Task sheet 2

Writing a playscript

Aim

To write and act out a playscript based on a modern-day retelling of Chapters 3 and 4 of *Treasure Island* by Robert Louis Stevenson.

Tasks

- Use the **My action planning sheet** to help you plan your work.

- **Discuss** with someone in your group your ideas for modernising the story. Use the **Story update sheet** to help you organise your ideas.

- **Read** Chapters 3 and 4 again and make a note of any important things the characters say.

- **Plan** your playscript and write your first draft (use a word processing program). Use the **Playscript guide** to help you. Remember to include stage directions.

- **Decide** what sort of set/costumes you will need. **Design** in detail the set for your play.

- **Practise** performing your script. **Edit** your script where you think it needs improving. Complete your final script.

- **Perform** your play!

Extension work

- Design a poster for your play. Think about how you would encourage people to come and watch it.

Planning guidelines

What to do

1. Read the task sheets carefully then make up your action plan of tasks to do and when to do them by completing the 'My action planning sheet'. Ask your teacher to help you with anything you are not sure of.

2. When reading the chapters, make a note of any words or phrases you do not understand. This will help you when you are discussing the language the author has used. You may need to read the text a couple of times to make sure you understand everything that is happening in the story.

3. Completing the 'Text map' and 'Incident line' sheets will help you understand the story better.

4. Think carefully about how you could set the story in today's world. How different would the setting and characters be? What things might stay the same? What things would definitely change? The 'Story update' sheet will help you plan out your ideas for your play.

5. Before you plan and write your script make sure you know how to set out a playscript correctly. Ask your teacher to help you.

6. The 'Resources' sheet will give you lots of ideas about where to find ideas and information for creating your play. Make sure you always ask your teacher's permission before you contact anyone or use the internet.

7. Choose a suitable word processing program to write and edit your script. Remember to include stage directions.

8. Design your set carefully so you have a detailed plan of what it will look like. You may be able to use ICT to do pictures and plans.

9. Practise your play, improve it and then arrange a time with your teacher to perform it. Good luck!

Resources

Internet and CD Roms	*The Hutchinson Multimedia Encyclopedia 2000* has entries that might be helpful: Treasure Island; Piracy. Find out the meaning of the following terms: dramaturgy; stage directions; exit; exeunt; stage; stage whisper. *Infopedia* (Future Publishing) has a section on: Language and Literature – Writers and Poets – Stevenson, R.L. For information about the book and access to the chapters, go to: *www.ukoln.ac.uk/services/treasure/setframe.htm*	Try other CD-Rom encyclopaedias
Speakers and other sources	A director from local theatre or amateur company. A set designer from theatre or drama company. A drama teacher or art teacher from a further education college.	Contact by writing or phoning.
Libraries	Reference books on how to stage a play might be helpful for ideas to use in your production.	The librarian will help you.
Visits	Arrange a backstage visit to a theatre when a play is being rehearsed. Arrange a trip to see a play at the theatre.	These can be individual or group visits. Discuss places to visit with friends.
Audience	Your year group and parents and teachers.	
Your own ideas	Discuss your ideas with friends, ask for their views on your ideas.	Discuss your ideas with friends and your teacher.

Text Map

Treasure Island

The plot

The Captain is ill – what does he want Jim to do?
Who is after the Captain?
What happens when the blind man visits the Captain?
What does Jim do?
How do Jim and his mother deal with the situation?
What happens at the Inn when the men arrive?

Language

This text was written in 1881 and set in the 1700s.
Make a list of the words and phrases which seem old-fashioned and are not used much today.

Incidents

There are several things that happen that keep the story developing - can you say what they are? How do they help make the story interesting?

Note all the things that happen on the incident line chart.

Chapters 3 and 4

Themes and issues

The Captain is ill - why does Jim give him rum?
Should Jim have told the doctor about Flint's crew?
The villagers refuse to help Jim and his mother. What do you think of their reasons for refusing? Should they have helped?
Jim and his mother open the Captain's chest and take some money - were they right to do this?

The setting

Where does the action take place?
What clues in the text tell us when the action took place?

Characters

Who tells the story?
What is the Captain like?
What sort of boy do you think Jim is?
What effect does the blind beggar have on the Captain?
How does Jim describe the beggar?
What does the reader learn about Jim's mother?

Incident line chart

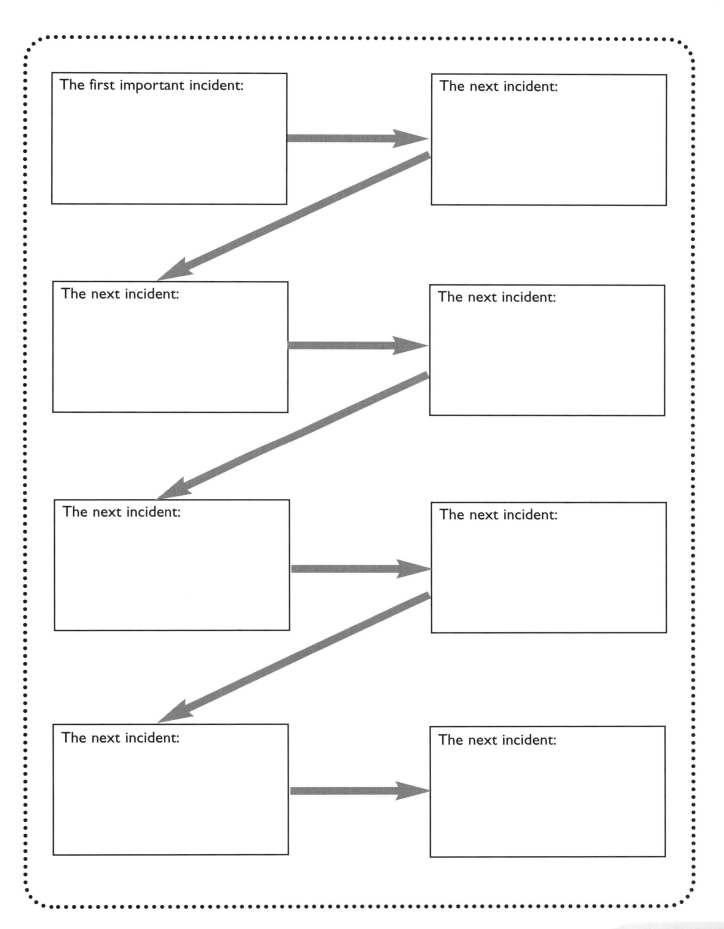

The first important incident:

The next incident:

The next incident:

The next incident:

The next incident:

The next incident:

The next incident:

The next incident:

Story update

How would you retell the story today?

Think about:
- the setting – how might this be different today?
- the characters – what sort of people might they be today?
- what happens (incidents) – how could you make the story believable if it happened today?

Then	Now
Setting:	**Setting:**
Characters:	**Characters:**
Incidents:	**Incidents:**

Playscript guide

Language

Think about:

How Jim, his mother, the doctor and the pirates (or a modern-day equivalent) would speak to each other.

What sort of language might they use?

Remember - you can only use language that is acceptable to your audience!

The scene

Plan who is in your scene – what they should say and do.

Use the scene to tell the audience what Jim is like and what difficulties he faces from the other characters.

Setting

Think carefully about the setting you design. The audience must believe that your play can take place in your setting.

Remember - a play is visual so make it interesting for the audience to look at.

My playscript

Time

The audience must understand the time in which the play is set. You can do this through costumes and in the words the characters use.

Incidents

Use your incidents sheet to help you think of things that might happen in today's world. Remember to make sure that the things that happen are believable.

Features of a playscript

The work is divided up into large sections called 'Acts' and into smaller sections called 'Scenes'.

The scene setting is written in italics. It tells us where the characters are and what props they will need.

The characters' names are written in capitals down the left hand side of the page. Next to each name is the dialogue they speak.

Sometimes words are written in brackets to indicate how the dialogue is spoken.

Stage directions are written in italics in brackets.

Challenge 2

Myths and legends

Teacher's notes

Purposes

- To explore how mythical characters are portrayed in literature and what their purpose is.

- To explore how characters in myths and legends have been developed over periods of time into familiar stereotypes.

- To investigate how modern writers use ancient stories to inform their own writing.

- To develop thinking, planning and time management skills.

Aims

- To read some text extracts about ancient myths and legends and write about them.

- To write a report comparing ancient mythical characters with modern-day ones.

Resources required

The pupil will need copies of the following:

1	'Challenge sheet'	page 143
2	'My action planning sheet'	page 144
3	'Task sheets'	pages 21 and 22
4	'Planning guidelines'	page 23
5	'Resources' sheet	page 24
6	'Comparison sheet'	page 25
7	'Character sheet'	page 26
8	'Good/bad characters map'	page 27
9	'Report guide'	page 28
10	Text extracts	pages 29–33
11	'Skills sheets'	pages 145–148

The teacher's role

1 Introducing the challenge

Write the following into the top box of a copy of the 'Challenge sheet' (page 143):

You are going to read some text extracts about characters in ancient myths and legends from different cultures.

You are then going to choose a modern-day book or film that has dragons/gods/monsters in it and write a report comparing ancient mythical characters with modern-day ones.

Then photocopy the 'Challenge sheet' and give it to the pupils. Alternatively, they could be given a blank copy of the sheet and write the challenge on it themselves. It is important for them to have the challenge to refer to.

2 Providing support for the task sheets

Reading the texts
Before sharing the texts, discuss with the pupils what they already know about the characters in ancient myths and legends. How many stories have they read before? From what cultures? What do these myths and legends have in common?

The extracts could be shared with the whole class, with the more able pupils then working in a group to carry out 'Task sheet 1' while the teacher continues to explore the texts with the rest of the class.

Act as a guide in the discussions of the texts to establish how the different writing is structured and what information is given about the characters in the text.

Using the 'Extract comparison' sheet
This sheet enables the pupils to make comparisons between the text extracts and introduces the idea that the texts come from different cultures.

Discuss with them what is the same and what is different about the extracts. Do they prefer to read information about mythical characters (as in The Dragon and Saint George) or do they prefer to read stories about them? Why?

Discuss what they found out in order to help them develop their ideas about myths and legends further. Why do they think different cultures have a tradition of myths and legends? How would they have been used by people in the past? How are these stories used today? Do people from different cultures have similar myths and legends?

Using the 'Character sheet'
This sheet enables the pupils to consider one creature/character in more depth. It is used in both

'Task sheets 1 and 2' to allow a comparison between an ancient mythical character and a modern-day one to be made. The pupils will need to refer to these sheets when they discuss stereotyping in 'Task sheet 2'.

Guide the pupils when they are selecting a modern-day book/film that has a dragon/god or monster in it. The following may be useful:

Films: 'Dragonheart' and 'Jason and the Argonauts'

Book: 'The Ringworld' books by Terry Pratchett

Using the 'Good and bad characters map' sheet
Completing this sheet will enable the pupils to investigate the ways good and bad characters are portrayed in stories. Discuss it with them, paving the way for discussions about stereotyping of characters. Do good characters always have particular qualities? How do authors usually portray bad characters? Do the characters in the text extracts and the modern-day story they have chosen fit these portrayals?

Display a list of the good and bad qualities of characters compiled from the discussion. This list could be used to compare how the pupils' ideas fit with their findings.

Using the 'Report guide'
This sheet can be used to help the pupils write their report as suggested in 'Task sheet 2'. It provides a framework to develop the formal piece of writing. Discuss the sheet with them to share ideas about the points made on it. Talk about how reports can be structured (introduction, conclusion, headings, sub-headings) and the correct tense to use.

Note: a useful teacher's site is:
http://www.dreamtime.net.au/teachers/uk.cfm
(It gives ideas on the use of myths and legend in pupils' work. Linked to National Curriculum.)

Links to the National Curriculum

English – Speaking and Listening

Level 4: Pupils listen and talk with increased confidence.
Ideas are developed thoughtfully.
Level 5: Questions are asked to develop ideas and take into account others' views.

English – Reading

Level 4: Understanding of characters is shown.
The text is referred to when explaining ideas.
Level 5: Sentences and phrases are selected to support views.
Key features in a text are identified.

English – Writing

Level 4: Ideas are sustained and developed.
Grammatically correct sentences are beginning to be used.
Level 5: Simple and complex sentences are organised into paragraphs.
Words with complex regular patterns are spelt correctly.
Punctuation is usually used accurately.
Handwriting is joined, clear and legible.

Links to Literacy Framework

Year 5, Term 2

Word level work

W3 – use dictionaries and IT spell-checks.

Sentence level work

S5 – to use punctuation effectively.

Text level work

T1 – to identify and classify the features of myths and legends.
T13 – to review and edit writing to produce a final form.
T22 – to plan, compose, edit and refine a comparative report.

Assessment sheet

Myths and legends

Name:_____ Date: _____

	Achieved	To achieve
Speaking and Listening:		

Speaking and Listening:

Level 4:
- Listens and talks with confidence.
- Ideas are developed thoughtfully.

Level 5:
- Questions are asked to develop ideas and make contributions that take others' views into account.

Reading:

Level 4:
- Understanding of characters is shown.
- Text is referred to when explaining ideas.

Level 5:
- Sentences and phrases are selected to support views.
- Key features are identified.

Writing:

Level 4:
- Ideas are sustained and developed.
- Grammatically complex sentences are beginning to be used.

Level 5:
- Simple and complex sentences are organised into paragraphs.
- Words with complex regular patterns are spelt correctly.
- Punctuation is usually used accurately.
- Handwriting is joined, clear and legible.

Task sheet 1

Reading the texts

Aim

To read some text extracts about ancient myths and legends and write about what you found out.

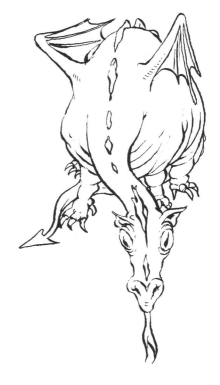

Tasks

- Use the **My action planning sheet** to help you plan your work.

- **Read** the text extracts through carefully.

- **Compare** the extracts by completing the **Comparison sheet** where you are asked to record:

  – the name of the country the extract is from;

  – whether the extract tells a story or gives you information;

  – the names of the characters in the extract;

  – what you have learned from reading it.

- **Share** what you have found out with other people in your group.

- **Choose one** character from any of the extracts. **Write** information about this character by completing the **Character sheet**.

Task sheet 2

Writing a report

Aim

To write a report that compares ancient mythical characters with modern-day ones.

Tasks

• Use the **My action planning sheet** to help you plan your work.

• **Choose** a modern-day book or film that has a dragon, a god or a monster in it. Ask your teacher to help you decide which character to choose.

• **Write** information about this character by completing the **Character sheet**.

• **Complete** the **Good/bad characters map sheet**.

• **Look up** the meaning of the word 'stereotype' in a dictionary. Discuss what you think it means with others in your group and with your teacher.

• **Discuss** this question with others in your group:

Do you think the character in your modern-day story/film is a stereotype of the same type of character found in ancient myths and legends?

• **Write a report** comparing your modern-day character with the same type of character in ancient myths and legends. Use the **Report guide** to help you.

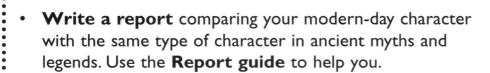

Extension work

• Find out about the myths and legends of different countries such as Africa, India and Scandinavia. Write about one that you like. Explain what it is about and why you like it.

Planning guidelines

What to do

1. Read the task sheets carefully then decide your action plan of tasks to do and when to do them by completing the 'My action planning sheet'. Ask your teacher to help you with anything you are not sure of.

2. When reading the text extracts, make a note of anything you do not understand. Use these notes to ask your teacher for any help you might need. You may need to read the texts a couple of times to make sure you understand everything that is happening in them.

3. Completing the 'Comparison sheet' will help you to keep a record of what each text was about. Share your ideas with others in your group.

4. Completing the 'Character sheet' for a character from the text extracts and a character from a modern-day book or film of your own choice will help you to make comparisons between the two characters.

5. Completing the 'Good/bad characters map' sheet will help you think more carefully about how authors present characters in their stories. It will also help you when you are discussing the term 'stereotyping' and what this means.

6. The 'Resources' sheet will give you lots of ideas about where to find ideas and information for writing your report. Make sure you always ask your teacher's permission before you contact anyone or use the internet.

7. The 'Report guide' will help you write your report. After you have written it, share it with someone in your group. Do they think you need to make any changes? Edit your report to improve it.

Resources

Internet	http://home.freeuk.net/elloughton13/theatre.htm www.perseus.tufts.edu/ www.loggia.com/myth/myth.html www.greekmythology.com	Try CD-Rom encyclopaedias
Speakers and other sources	Writers of books may come and talk about their books and characters or answer letters/e-mails about their texts. Local historians may know about local myths and legends.	Contact by writing or phoning – ask your teacher first.
Libraries	Libraries will have old and modern texts for you to choose to read for Task Sheet 2. Non-fiction books on the subject may also be available.	The librarian will help you.
Visits	Local places where there are legends from the past may be interesting to visit. Museums may have information and displays.	These can be individual or group visits. Discuss places to visit with friends.
Audience	Your friends and your teacher will be your audience.	
Your own ideas	Discuss these with your friends and your teacher.	Discuss your ideas with friends and your teacher.

Comparison sheet

extract	country of origin	Is it a story or information?	characters' names	what I have learned from reading this text
Medusa				
The stolen hammer of Thor				
The Dragon and Saint George				

Character sheet

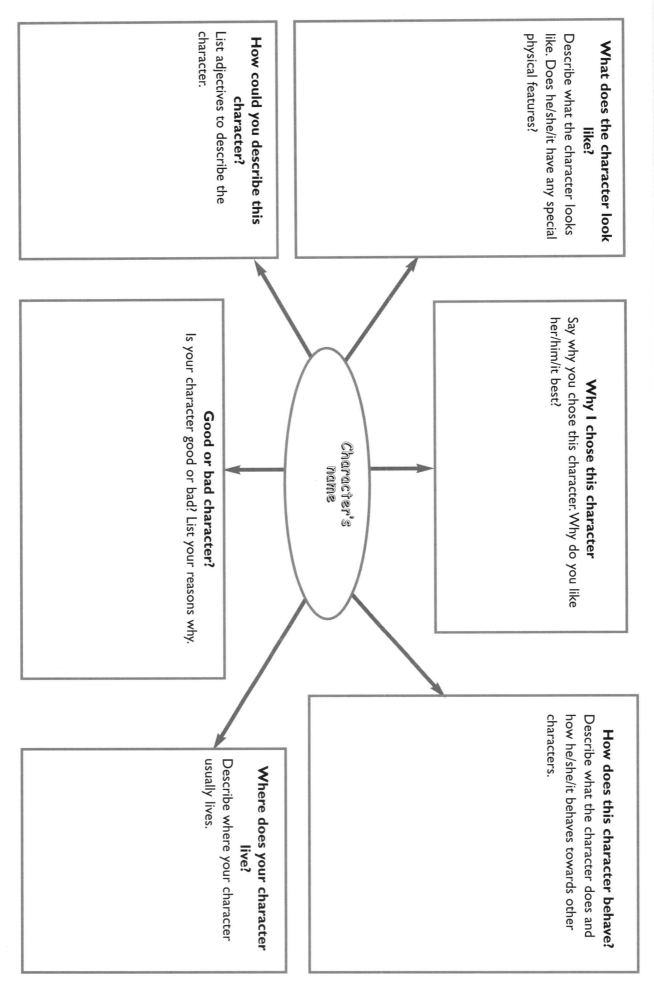

What does the character look like?

Describe what the character looks like. Does he/she/it have any special physical features?

How could you describe this character?

List adjectives to describe the character.

Why I chose this character

Say why you chose this character. Why do you like her/him/it best?

Character's name

Good or bad character?

Is your character good or bad? List your reasons why.

How does this character behave?

Describe what the character does and how he/she/it behaves towards other characters.

Where does your character live?

Describe where your character usually lives.

Myths and legends

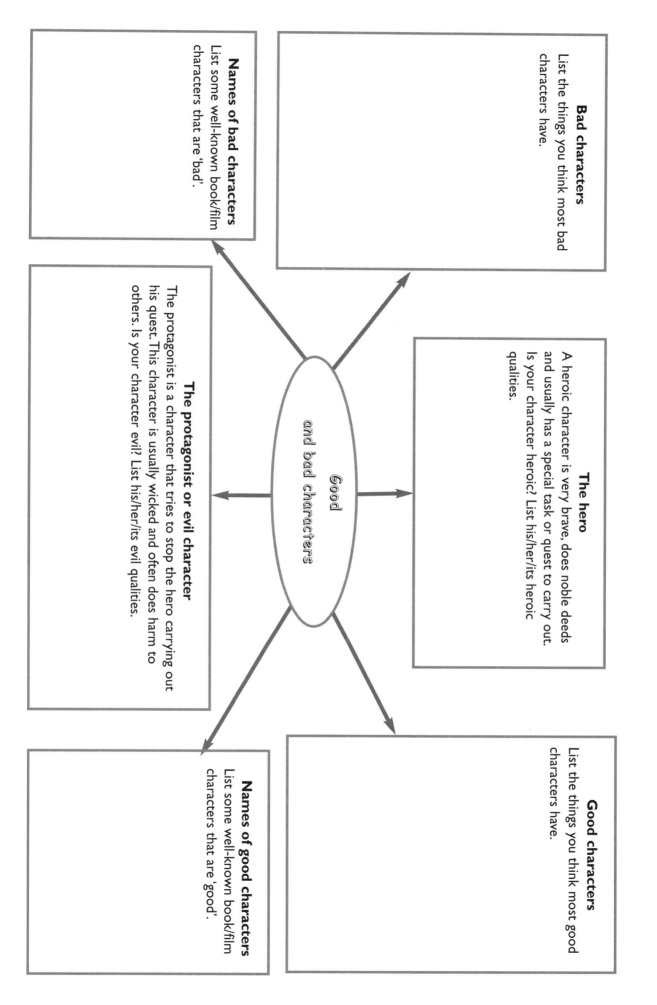

Bad characters

List the things you think most bad characters have.

Names of bad characters

List some well-known book/film characters that are 'bad'.

Good and bad characters

The hero

A heroic character is very brave, does noble deeds and usually has a special task or quest to carry out. Is your character heroic? List his/her/its heroic qualities.

The protagonist or evil character

The protagonist is a character that tries to stop the hero carrying out his quest. This character is usually wicked and often does harm to others. Is your character evil? List his/her/its evil qualities.

Good characters

List the things you think most good characters have.

Names of good characters

List some well-known book/film characters that are 'good'.

Myths and legends

Features of a report

present tense

third person

non chronological organisation

factual writing

Purpose

Why are you writing the report?

What do you want the reader to learn?

Things to think about:

Decide whether you will use headings or not (such as introduction, headings for different paragraphs and conclusion)

A report gives the reader information about something.

Your report is going to compare the way ancient mythical characters are portrayed with the same type of characters in modern-day stories or films.

My report

Introduction

The introduction should tell the reader what you are going to write about.

Explain which type of character you have chosen to write about – a dragon, a god or a monster.

Development

After the introduction write about the following points:

How your chosen character has been portrayed in ancient myths and legends.

How your chosen character has been portrayed in modern-day stories.

Conclusion

Finally, tell the reader whether or not you think modern writers' characters are based on characters from ancient stories and whether or not you think the characters are stereotyped.

Text extract

from *The Kingfisher Book of Myths and Legends*

Medusa

Athene had not only told Perseus how to destroy the Gorgon, she had given him the means. He now carried her brightly polished shield in one hand and his sword in the other.

He knew that he must be getting close to Medusa's cave. The valley in which he stood was filled with stone people, some trapped as they turned to run, others frozen in horror, their mouths open, the screams still on their lips. It was as if they had been photographed in the last second of their life. Their reaction in that second had been caught for eternity. One young soldier had covered his face, but then he had tried to peep through his fingers. His stone hand still shuttered his stone eyes. A local government official stood rigid with a puzzled smile, his stone fingers clutching a scrap of yellowing paper. There were stone women and stone children. It was like a crazy open-air museum.

Now Perseus saw the mouth of a large cave, yawning darkly at him. Holding the shield more tightly than ever, he climbed up the gentle slope and, taking a deep breath, entered the gloom.

"Medusa!" he called out. His voice sounded lost in the shadows.

Something moved at the back of the cave.

"Medusa!" he repeated.

Now he could hear breathing and the sound of hissing.

"I am Perseus!" he announced.

"Perseus!" came a deep, throaty voice from the back of the cave. It was followed by a horrible giggling. "Have you come to see me?"

The Gorgon stepped forward into the light.

Medusa (cont)

For a dreadful moment, Perseus was tempted to look up at her, to meet her eyes. But with all his strength he kept his head turned away as Athene had instructed him and instead of looking at Medusa he looked at her reflection in the shield. Now he could see her green skin, her poisonous red eyes and her yellow teeth, all reflected in the polished bronze. He lifted the sword.

"Look at me! Look at me!" the Gorgon cried.

Still he kept his eyes on the shield. He took another step into the cave. Now the reflection was huge, the teeth snarling at him out of the shield. The snakes writhed furiously, hissing with the sound of red hot needles being plunged into water.

"Look at me! Look at me!"

How could he find her when all he could see was the reflection? Surely it would be easier to kill her if he took just one quick look at her, just to make sure that he didn't miss…

"Yes. That's right. Look at me!"

"No!"

With a despairing cry, Perseus swung wildly with his sword. He felt the sharp steel bite into flesh and bone. The Gorgon screamed. The snakes exploded around her head as the whole thing flew from her shoulders, bounced against the cave wall and rolled to the ground. A fountain of blood spouted out of her neck as her body crumpled. Then at last it was over. Still not looking at it, Perseus picked up the grim trophy of his victory and dropped it into a heavy sack.

Text extract

from *The Kingfisher Book of Myths and Legends*

THE STOLEN HAMMER OF THOR

What we call Thursday was originally called Thor's day, for it was dedicated by the Vikings to Thor, the god of thunder and son of Odin, who was himself king of the gods. Tall and strong, with a flowing red beard, Thor lived with his father in the citadel of Asgard which could only be reached by crossing a rainbow bridge. It was said by the Vikings that the sound of thunder was nothing more than the wheels of Thor's chariot rumbling over the clouds.

Thor possessed a pair of iron gloves and a magic belt that doubled his strength. His voice was so loud that it could be heard even above the clamour of a battle and would have his enemies fainting with terror. But his most prized possession was his hammer – Mjolnir the Destroyer. Mjolnir had been made from a meteorite that had fallen to the earth during a storm. It had been fashioned into shape by a dwarf whose skill in ironwork was unrivalled. Using his strength, Thor could hurl the hammer at a target on the other side of the world. Never did it miss its mark. Once thrown, it always returned to his hand. Every year, Thor used Mjolnir to break up the ice of winter in order to allow spring to come once again.

You can imagine, then, how Thor felt when he woke up one day to find that his precious hammer was missing. He looked under his pillow, then under his bed. He tore the pillow to shreds, then the bed to matchwood. Finally, he ransacked every room in the house, knocking down several walls with his bare fists – but all to no avail.

It was then that Loki, the god of firelight, happened to pass. Seeing Thor sitting in the street with half the contents of the house and, indeed, half the house itself scattered around him, he asked what was the matter.

Now Loki was a sly, untrustworthy god who delighted in mischief. Normally Thor wouldn't have trusted him as far as he could throw him (which was actually a very long way indeed) but by now he was so desperate, he told him everything.

THE STOLEN HAMMER OF THOR (cont)

"Don't worry, my dear fellow," Loki said. "I'll find Mjolnir for you. I expect one of the giants has stolen it."

"The giants!" Thor's face lit up. "Why didn't I think of that?"

"I can't imagine." Loki smiled to himself, for he did not think very highly of Thor's intelligence. "You wait here. I'll see what I can do."

With that, Loki turned himself into a bird and flew out of Asgard, over the rainbow bridge and on to the frozen land of Jotunheim where the giants lived. Loki was sure he would find the hammer there, for the giants had never liked the gods and they actively hated Thor who had killed many of their number. But he was unsuccessful. Three times he flew around Jotunheim and he spied nothing. At last he settled beside a lake where, despite the ice that floated on the surface, one of the giants was swimming.

"Having a good swim, your majesty?" he asked, for the giant was none other than Thrym, King of Jotunheim.

"Not cold enough," Thrym replied, although his skin was quite blue and his beard had frozen solid. "What brings you to Jotunheim, Loki?"

"A hammer," Loki replied. "Thor's hammer, to be precise."

At that, Thryn roared with laughter. "So he sent you, did he? Well, let me tell you something, my friend. You'll never find it!"

"So you know where it is?" Loki said.

"Of course I do. I was the one who stole it! And now I've hidden it eight fathoms underground, and only I know where."

Once again the giant burst into laughter, icy drops of water splashing out of his hair.

Text extract

from *Folk Tales of the British Isles*

THE DRAGON AND SAINT GEORGE

THERE are no dragons today – mainly thanks to the knights
and heroes who so thoughtlessly rode about the place killing
them off. This is a pity, for dragons must have been
astonishing creatures; part snake and part crocodile, with bits
of lion, eagle and hawk thrown in for good measure. Not only
could they leap into the air and fly (a tremendous feat when
you think how heavy their scales must have been) but they
could also run at great speed. Not that a dragon would ever
run away. Dragons were generally very brave creatures.
When they were angry or frightened, smoke would come
hissing out of their nostrils. When things got really rough,
flames would rush out of their mouths. But there was no such thing as a cowardly
dragon.

Only the Chinese understood and admired the dragon. It was often said that some of the
greatest Chinese emperors had been born the sons of dragons. Dragon bones and teeth
were used as medicine. A dragon guarded the houses of the Chinese gods and brought
rain to the earth when the crops needed it. That is why the Chinese still fly dragon kites
and honour the dragon by including paper models of it in their New Year celebrations.
The Chinese really did like the dragon.

But in fourth century Palestine – when Saint George was born – dragons were more
feared than admired. It is true that they did have some unsettling habits. They tended to
live in rather dank and nasty caves, for example, often guarding huge piles of treasure

which had almost certainly been stolen from somebody else.
They also had an unhealthy appetite for human flesh, their
favourite food being princesses – although any young woman
would do. But they were not the only man-eating animal on
the globe. It was just that they got all the bad publicity.

Anyway, Saint George was the most famous dragon-killer of
all – which is strange because he never actually killed a
dragon. The other strange thing is that he really was born in
Palestine, even though he later became the patron saint of
England.

Challenge 3

Narrative poetry

Teacher's notes

Purposes

- To understand that stories can be told through poems.
- To identify the themes, story and characters in poems.
- To analyse pieces of writing and adapt it for different purposes and audiences.
- To use ICT to present a finished product.
- To develop thinking, planning and time management skills.

Aims

- To read some classical narrative poems and write about one of them in more detail.
- To write a newspaper report based on the story from a classical narrative poem.

Resources required

The pupil will need copies of the following:

1	'Challenge sheet'	page 143
2	'My action planning sheet'	page 144
3	'Task sheets'	pages 37 and 38
4	'Planning guidelines'	page 39
5	'Resources' sheet	page 40
6	'Discussion sheet'	page 41
7	'Writing guide'	page 42
8	'Newspaper report guide'	page 43
9	Poems	pages 44–46
10	'Skills sheets'	pages 145–148

The teacher's role

1 Introducing the challenge

Write the following into the top box of a copy of the 'Challenge' sheet (page 143):

You are going to read some classical poems that tell a story.

You are then going to choose one of the poems and find out more about it in order to write a newspaper report based on the poem.

Then photocopy the 'Challenge sheet' and give it to the pupils. Alternatively, they could be given a blank copy of the sheet and write the challenge on it themselves. It is important for them to have the challenge to refer to.

2 Providing support for the task sheets

Reading the poems

Before sharing the poems, discuss with the pupils what they already know about narrative poems. Have they read poems that tell a story before? Which narrative poems do they already know? How does a story told in a poem differ from one told in a fiction book?

Explain that they will be reading three poems by some well-known poets – Robert Browning (1812–1889), Robert Southey (1774–1843) and Charles Wolfe (1791–1823). Have they read any poems by these poets before? What do they know about these poets?

About the poems

'from The Pied Piper of Hamelin' is an extract from a long narrative poem that tells the story of the mysterious disappearance of the children of Hamelin many years ago. Robert Browning wants to show us the power of the piper's flute; the excitement the children felt when they heard him playing and the fear of the adults when they saw their children following him and could not stop them. There are various explanations of the beginnings of the legend of the Pied Piper of Hamelin. The pupils could be encouraged to investigate them.

'The Inchcape Rock' relates the story of the fate of the pirate, Sir Ralph the Rover, whose evil act eventually leads to the destruction of his ship and the death of himself and his crew. Robert Southey uses descriptions of the weather to help set the scene for the story to unfold. He describes two different scenes in the same place. (The pupils should be encouraged to look at the scene and mood at the beginning of the poem and compare this with the ending – they are very different.)

'The Burial of Sir John Moore after Corunna' describes how a real historical character was buried after he died in battle in Greece. Charles Wolfe shows how difficult the soldiers find the task of burying their leader. He describes their thoughts and feelings. He shows us that the soldiers cared for their leader and thought him to be a hero. (The pupils could be encouraged to find out about Sir John Moore and the battle of Corunna.)

The poems could be shared with the class with everyone carrying out the activities on 'Task sheet 1'. The more able pupils should be able to carry out the work independently while the teacher leads the discussions with the others.

Using the 'Discussion sheet'

This sheet enables the pupils to make a detailed study of one of the poems. It helps them to focus on the themes, characters and plot of the story as well as consider the techniques the poet has used to create images in the reader's mind through his use of language. The more able pupils could work in pairs to complete this sheet.

Ask the pupils what the poem is about and lead the discussion about any themes or issues that appear in the poems. It is important that the ideas/images the words give us are also discussed.

Using the 'Writing guide'

At the end of 'Task sheet 1', the pupils are required to write in more detail about one of the poems. The 'Writing guide' can be used to help them do this. It requires them to use the information they have gathered from completing the 'Discussion sheet' to help them explain what they think the poem is about and why they like it.

Remind the pupils to make notes for each part of the piece of writing (introduction, development and conclusion) and to use the 'Writing guide' to help them with their planning.

Using the 'Newspaper guide'

This sheet will help the pupils to plan and write their newspaper report. Explain how newspaper reports should answer the questions: who, when, what, why and how. Practice in reading and identifying the answers to these questions using a collection of reports from the local newspaper will help them to understand how a newspaper report is written.

Microsoft Publisher can be used to create a newspaper page.

Links to the National Curriculum

English – Speaking and Listening

Level 4: In discussion pupils are responsive to others' views. They take turns in discussion.
Level 5: Pupils show that they can respond to others' views and ideas.

English – Reading

Level 4: Pupils show understanding of ideas, characters and themes in the texts.

They read fluently and with understanding.
Level 5: Pupils show understanding of texts and select relevant phrases, words and information from a variety of texts.

English – Writing

Level 4: Pupils organise writing appropriately for the purpose of the reader.
Level 5: Pupils convey meaning clearly in a range of forms.

History

Level 4: Pupils organise writing appropriately for the purpose of the reader.
Level 5: Pupils convey meaning in a range of forms.

ICT

Level 4: Pupils use ICT to present different forms of information for an intended audience.
Pupils work with others to explore a variety of information sources.
Level 5: Pupils use ICT to refine and present information.

Links to Literacy Framework

Year 5, Term 2

Word level work

W3 – use dictionaries and IT spell-checks.

Sentence level work

S2 – to consolidate the basic conventions of standard English.
S3 – to understand how writing can be adapted for different audiences and purposes.

Text level work

T4 – to read a range of narrative poems.
T10 – to understand the differences between literal and figurative language.
T13 – to review and edit writing to produce a final form.
T17 – to locate information confidently and efficiently.
T22 – to plan, compose, edit and refine short non-chronological reports using reading as a source.
T24 – to evaluate their work.

Assessment sheet

Name:_____ Date: _____

	Achieved	To achieve
Speaking and Listening: **Level 4:** • In discussion he/she is responsive to others' views. • He/she can take turns in discussion. **Level 5:** • He/she can show that they respond to others' views and ideas. (Can justify ideas and views.)		
Reading: **Level 4:** • Shows understanding of ideas and themes. • Reads fluently. **Level 5:** • He/she shows understanding of texts and selects relevant phrases, words and information from a variety of sources.		
Writing: **Level 4:** • Can organise writing appropriately for the purpose of the reader. **Level 5:** • Can convey meaning clearly in a range of forms.		
History: **Level 4:** • Can find out about events and people. Can describe some of the main events, people and changes. **Level 5:** • Can use knowledge and understanding to evaluate and use information.		
ICT: **Level 4:** • Can use ICT to present different forms of information for an intended audience. • Can work with others to explore a variety of information sources. **Level 5:** • Can use ICT to refine and present information.		

Task sheet 1

Investigating how stories are told in poems

Aim

To read some classical narrative poems and write about one of them in more detail.

Tasks

- Use the **My action planning sheet** to help you plan your work.

- **Read** the poems carefully. Choose the poem you like best.

- **Discuss** with a partner the themes, story and characters of your chosen poem. Use the **Discussion sheet** to help you.

- Then **write** about your chosen poem. Write what the poem is about and why you like it. Use the **Writing guide** to help you.

Think about:

   – what the poem is about;

   – why you like the poem;

   – how the poet uses language to create images and to tell a story;

   – how the poet uses words that appeal to our senses;

   – what you have learned from reading the poem.

Task sheet 2

Writing a newspaper report

Aim

To write a newspaper report based on the story from a classical narrative poem.

Tasks

- Use the **My action planning sheet** to help you plan your work.

- **Read** out one verse of your chosen poem (the one you chose for Task sheet 1) to a partner or the rest of your group. Tell them why you chose this poem in particular.

- **Discuss** with others in your group what you think makes a good newspaper story.

- **Find out** if any of the facts in your poem are true. Use the **Resources sheet** to help you decide where you might go to find information.

- **Plan** a newspaper story based on your poem. Use the **Newspaper guide** to help you write it.

- **Select** a suitable **computer program** to set out your story in a newspaper format. Decide on the heading, sub-headings and illustrations you will use.

- **Edit** your report to improve it before printing out a final version.

Extension work

- Make up a narrative poem which tells the story of a boy or girl who go on a day trip to a place you have been to. Write three to four verses which have four lines each.

Planning guidelines

What to do

1. Read the task sheets carefully then make up your action plan of tasks to do and when to do them by completing the 'My action planning sheet'. Ask your teacher to help you with anything you are not sure of.

2. When reading the poems, make a note of anything you do not understand. Use these notes to ask your teacher for any help you might need. You may need to read the poems a couple of times to make sure you understand everything that is happening in them.

3. Completing the 'Discussion sheet' with a partner will help you to understand what the poem is about and how the poet has used language to describe what is happening to the reader. Share what you found out with your teacher.

4. The 'Writing guide' will help you write about your chosen poem in more detail. Your teacher will help you plan out your writing. Share your finished writing with others in your group. Do they agree with what you have found out?

5. Before planning your newspaper report, make sure you understand what makes a good newspaper story. Read some stories in your local newspaper first to help you.

6. The 'Resources sheet' will give you lots of ideas about where to find information about your chosen poem. You need to find out if any of the facts mentioned in the poem are true. Make sure you always ask your teacher's permission before you contact anyone or use the internet.

7. The 'Newspaper report guide' will help you write your report. Make sure you select a computer program that is suitable for setting out your story like a real newspaper.

8. After you have written your report, share it with someone in your group. Do they think you need to make any changes? Edit your report to improve it and then print out a final version.

Resources

Internet	An account of the battle of Corunna: *http://www.britishbattles.com/peninsula/peninsula-coruna.htm* Poetry of Charles Wolfe: *http://eir.library.utoronto.ca/rpo/display/poem2327.html* Inchcape Rock: *http://10.1911encyclopedia.org/B/BE/BELL_or_INCHCAPE_ROCK.htm* The Pied Piper: *http://www.ims.uni-stuttgart.de/~jonas/piedpiper.html* *http://www.deproverbio.com/DPjournal/DP,5,2,99/MIEDER/PIPER.htm*	Try CD-Rom encyclopaedias
Speakers and other sources	A poet who visits schools could be helpful in explaining how imagery is used in poetry. Newspaper archives, such as of *The Times* may have material about 'The Battle of Corunna'. The local authority where the rock was may help with information about the 'Inchcape Rock'.	Contact by writing or phoning – ask your teacher first.
Libraries	Poetry books, encyclopaedias and general information texts may be available.	The librarian will help you.
Visits	A local War Museum may have artefacts that show what war was like at the time of 'The Battle of Corunna'.	These can be individual or group visits. Discuss places to visit with friends.
Audience	Your group, teacher and peers.	
Your own ideas	Discuss your ideas with your teacher and group. Try to organise and research your ideas.	

Narrative poetry

Discussion sheet

Title of poem_____

The story

How does the story begin?

List the events in the story to show how it develops.

How does the story end?

Characters

Who are the important characters?

What are they like?

Theme

A theme is an idea that runs through the poem.

What ideas does the poem give you?

Find lines in the poem that show these ideas.

Language

List the words used that describe what is happening.

List the words that give the reader a picture of the scene.

What did you enjoy about the poem?

Writing guide

Narrative poetry

Use of language

Explain how words are used which appeal to our senses.

What sort of images do we see when we read the poem?

Give two or three examples from the poem.

Remember

Check that:

Your sentences make sense;

You have written in paragraphs;

You have checked your spelling and punctuation.

Things to think about:

Use the discussion sheet to remind you what the poem is about.

Poem

A narrative piece of writing tells the reader a story. It may be true or made up. It can be written in sentences or as a poem.

Introduction

The introduction should tell the reader what you are going to write about.

Say what the poem is about and what the poet is telling the reader.

Development

After the introduction write about what the poet wants us to think about when we read the poem.

Give examples from the poem of how he uses words and images to make us understand the poem.

Conclusion

Explain what you think of the poem.

What did you learn from it?

Why do you like it?

Narrative poetry

Features of a newspaper report

bold, catchy heading

answers the questions who, where, when, what, why and how

past tense

third person

chronological organisation

factual writing

emotive language

Purpose

Why are you writing the report?

What do you want the reader to learn?

A newspaper report gives the reader information about an event that has happened.

You are going to write a newspaper report based on the story from the classical poem you have chosen.

My newspaper report

Things to think about

How you can make the headline grab the reader's attention.

The facts you want the reader to know about (make a list of them).

The picture(s) you will include.

The caption you will write to go with the picture.

How you will make the story exciting for the reader.

The computer program you will use to set out your report in a newspaper format.

Introduction

The introduction should tell the reader who the story is about and when it happened.

Development

After the introduction write about what happened, how it happened and why it happened.

Conclusion

Say how the people reacted to the event and how things ended.

The Burial of Sir John Moore after Corunna

by Charles Wolfe

Not a drum was heard, not a funeral note,
As his corse to the rampart we hurried;
Not a soldier discharged his farewell shot
O'er the grave where our hero we buried.

We buried him darkly at dead of night,
The sods with our bayonets turning,
By the struggling moonbeam's misty light
And the lanthorn dimly burning.

No useless coffin enclosed his breast,
Not in sheet or in shroud we wound him;
But he lay like a warrior taking his rest
With his martial cloak around him.

Few and short were the prayers we said,
And we spoke not a word of sorrow;
But we steadfastly gazed on the face that was dead,
And we bitterly thought of the morrow.

We thought, as we hollowed his narrow bed
And smoothed down his lonely pillow,
That the foe and the stranger would tread o'er his head,
And we far away on the billow!

Lightly they'll talk of the spirit that's gone,
And o'er his cold ashes upbraid him –
But little he'll reck, if they let him sleep on
In the grave where a Briton has laid him

But half of our heavy task was done
When the clock struck the hour for retiring;
And we heard the distant and random gun
That the foe was sullenly firing.

Slowly and sadly we laid him down,
From the field of his fame fresh and gory;
We carved not a line, and we raised not a stone,
But we left him alone with his glory.

Poem

The Inchcape Rock
by Robert Southey

No stir in the air, no stir in the sea,
The ship was as still as she could be;
Her sails from heaven received no motion,
Her keel was steady in the ocean.

Without either sign or sound of their shock,
The waves flowed over the Inchcape Rock;
So little they rose, so little they fell,
They did not move the Inchcape bell.

The Abbot of Aberbrothok
Had placed that bell on the Inchcape Rock;
On a buoy in the storm it floated and swung,
And over the waves its warning rung.

When the rock was hid by the surge's swell,
The mariners heard the warning bell:
And then they knew the perilous rock,
And blessed the Abbot of Aberbrothok.

The sun in heaven was shining gay,
All things were joyful on that day;
The sea-birds screamed as they wheeled
    around,
And there was joyance in their sound.

The buoy of the Inchcape bell was seen,
A darker speck on the ocean green;
Sir Ralph the Rover walked his deck,
And he fixed his eye on the darker speck.

He felt the cheering power of spring,
It made him whistle, it made him sing;
His heart was mirthful to excess –
But the Rover's mirth was wickedness.

His eye was on the Inchcape float:
Quoth he, 'My men, put out the boat,
And row me to the Inchcape Rock
And I'll plague the Abbot of Aberbrothok.'

The boat is lowered, the boatmen row,
And to the Inchcape Rock they go;
Sir Ralph bent over from the boat,
And he cut the bell from the Inchcape float.

Down sunk the bell with a gurgling sound –
The bubbles rose and burst around;
Quoth Sir Ralph, 'The next who comes to the
    Rock
Won't bless the Abbot of Aberbrothok.'

Sir Ralph the Rover sailed away;
He scoured the seas for many a day;
And, now grown rich with plundered store,
He steers his course for Scotland's shore.

So thick a haze o'erspreads the sky
They cannot see the sun on high;
The wind hath blown a gale all day,
At evening it hath died away.

On the deck the Rover takes his stand,
So dark it is they see no land.
Quoth Sir Ralph, 'It will be lighter soon,
For there is the dawn of the rising moon.'

'Canst hear', said one, 'the breakers roar?
For methinks we should be near the shore.
Now where we are we cannot tell,
But I wish I could hear the Inchcape Bell.'

They hear no sound – the swell is strong;
Though the wind hath fallen they drift along
Till the vessel strikes with a shivering shock –
'Oh! Heavens! it is the Inchcape Rock!'

Sir Ralph the Rover tore his hair,
And curst himself in his despair:
The waves rush in on every side,
The ship is sinking beneath the tide.

But even in his dying fear,
One dreadful sound could the Rover hear –
A sound as if, with the Inchcape bell,
The Devil below was ringing his knell.

Poem

from *The Pied Piper of Hamelin*

by Robert Browning

Once more he stept into the street;
And to his lips again
Laid his long pipe of smooth straight cane;
And ere he blew three notes (such sweet
Soft notes as yet musician's cunning
Never gave the enraptured air)
There was a rustling that seem'd like a
      bustling
Of merry crowds justling at pitching and
      hustling,
Small feet were pattering, wooden shoes
      clattering,
Little hands clapping, and little tongues
      chattering,
And, like fowls in a farm-yard when barley
      is scattering.
Out came the children running,
All the little boys and girls,
With rosy cheeks and flaxen curls,
And sparkling eyes and teeth like pearls,
Tripping and skipping, ran merrily after
The wonderful music with shouting and
      laughter.

The Mayor was dumb, and the Council
      stood
As if they were changed into blocks of
      wood,
Unable to move a step, or cry
To the children merrily skipping by –
And could only follow with the eye
That joyous crowd at the Piper's back.
But how the Mayor was on the rack,
And the wretched Council's bosoms beat,
As the Piper turn'd from the High Street
To where the Weser roll'd its waters
Right in the way of their sons and
      daughters!

However, he turned from south to west,
And to Koppelberg Hill his steps address'd,
And after him the children press'd;
Great was the joy in every breast.

"He never can cross that mighty top!
"He's forced to let the piping drop,
"And we shall see our children stop!"
When, lo, as they reach'd the mountain's side.
A wondrous portal open'd wide,
As if a cavern was suddenly hollow'd;
And the Piper advanced and the children
      follow'd,
And when all were in to the very last,
The door in the mountain-side shut fast.
Did I say all? No! One was lame,
And could not dance the whole of the way,
And in after years, if you would blame
His sadness, he was used to say,
"It's dull in our town since my playmates left!
I can't forget that I'm bereft
Of all the pleasant sights they see,
Which the Piper also promised me,
For he led us, he said, to a joyous land,
Joining the town and just at hand,
Where waters gush'd and fruit trees grew,
And flowers put forth a fairer hue,
And everything was strange and new;
The sparrows were brighter than peacocks
      here,
And the dogs outran our fallow deer,
And honey-bees had lost their stings,
And horses were born with eagles' wings;
And just as I became assured
My lame foot would be speedily cured,
The music stopp'd, and I stood still,
And found myself outside the Hill,
Left alone against my will,
To go now limping as before,
And never hear of the country more!"

46 **Literacy**
Challenges

Science fiction

Teacher's notes

Purposes

- To compare similar texts written in different decades.

- To analyse the features and writing styles of texts and to compare their content and vocabulary.

- To compare how science fiction writers present scientific ideas to their readers.

- To use ICT to present a finished product.

- To develop thinking, planning and time management skills.

Aims

- To identify the features of some science fiction texts and compare their content.

- To write a science fiction story that shows how a scientific discovery may be used in the future.

Resources required

The teacher will need to provide the pupil with a photocopy of the following:

1	'Challenge' sheet	page 143
2	'My action planning sheet'	page 144
3	'Task sheets'	pages 51 and 52
4	'Planning Guidelines'	page 53
5	'Resources' sheet	page 54
6	'Story map' sheet	page 55
7	'Information sheet'	page 56
8	'Science fiction story guide'	page 57
9	Text extracts	pages 58–65
10	'Isaac Asimov' sheet	page 66
11	'Skills sheets'	pages 145–148

The teacher's role

1 Introducing the challenge

Write the following into the top box of a copy of the 'Challenge' sheet (page 143):

You are going to read some science fiction texts and make some comparisons between them.

You are then going to write your own science fiction story that shows how a scientific discovery may be used in the future.

Then photocopy the 'Challenge sheet' and give it to the pupils. Alternatively, they could be given a blank copy of the sheet and write the challenge on it themselves. It is important for them to have the challenge to refer to.

2 Providing support for the task sheets

Reading the texts

Before sharing the texts, discuss with the pupils what they already know about science fiction stories. Have they read any before? Do they like these types of stories? Why/why not? Do they know any well-known science fiction authors? What is different about science fiction stories compared with other stories?

Explain that they will be reading four text extracts written by different authors writing at different times in history.

K A Applegate was born in 1956 and lives in North Carolina. A biography about him can be found at www.scholastic.com/kaaapplegate/about.htm.

A C Clarke was born in 1917. He wrote The Sentinel *in 1948 for a BBC competition (which he did not win). It is a short story which was developed into* 2001: A Space Odyssey *in which man is seen as an experiment trying to understand his place in the cosmos.*

Isaac Asimov (1920–1992) wrote a lot of science fiction. He established three laws of robotics:

1 A robot may not injure a human, or, through inaction, allow a human to come to harm;

2 A robot must obey the laws given it by humans except where such orders would conflict with the first law;

3 A robot must protect its own existence as long as such protection does not conflict with the first or second law.

These laws are applied in other science fiction books and films. The text extract from I Robot *(the 'Isaac Asimov' sheet) shows how he felt about how the ideas science fiction writers have can turn into fact at a later date.*

Have the pupils read any stories by these authors before? What do they know about these authors?

About the extracts

All the text extracts are from short stories.

Animorphs – The Illusion is from a series of books that feature Jake, Rachel, Tobias, Cassie, Marco and Ax, Animorphs who are fighting a desperate battle against the invasion of parasitic aliens called the Yeerks.

The Sentinel is about the discovery of a black obelisk that has been there for millions of years. It watches man and its makers know when man is sufficiently advanced to make contact.

An Ape About the House is about how people deal with animals as servants.

Little Lost Robot deals with a robot that appears to be breaking the first law of robotics; modifying the law has allowed it to let a human be killed. The use of language in rules and how we understand and follow rules is important in this story.

The 'Resources' sheet gives website addresses that can provide more information about the writers.

The extracts could be shared with the class as a whole with everyone carrying out the activities on 'Task sheet 1'. The more able pupils should be able to carry out the work independently while the teacher leads the discussions with the rest of the class.

Questions that could be asked include:
• 'What can you, as a reader, pick out that shows the texts are science fiction?'
• 'How do the stories differ? How are they the same?'
• 'Can you pick out the scientific ideas? Do they seem believable?'

Using the 'Story map' sheet
This sheet enables the pupils to make a detailed study of the texts. It enables them to focus on the setting, characters and plot of the story as well as consider the language used by the author.

The teacher's role is to choose one of the texts and guide the pupils through using the sheet, modelling for them how to use information from the text. The pupils could then work in pairs to complete the work on the remaining texts.

Using the 'Information sheet'
This sheet enables the pupils to make a more detailed comparison between the four texts in order to determine the scientific content of each one. After completing it, the pupils should be able to discover some of the features

science fiction texts have in common, such as the inclusion of scientific equipment/technical terms, writing about the future and the incorporation of scientific information.

The teacher could work through one extract with the pupils to ensure that they are finding the information needed. Skimming and scanning skills can be revisited and used in this task.

Using the 'Science fiction story guide'
This sheet will help the pupils plan and write their science fiction story. They may want to work in pairs initially to help each other plan a story plot and think up suitable scientific equipment and terms.

The teacher could use a film extract as a stimulus for 'Task sheet 2' in order to develop discussions about how science is presented to the viewer.

The story should be word processed to develop ICT skills. The teacher may need to show the pupils how to insert pictures from scanning or using clip art.

The teacher should discuss the sheet with the pupils before they begin their planning work and check that they are following the guidelines as they plan their ideas.

Links to the National Curriculum
English – Speaking and Listening
Level 4: Pupils' talk is adapted to the purpose and they convey their opinions clearly.
Level 5: Pupils talk using vocabulary that is appropriate to the purpose. They collect ideas together, evaluate them and come to conclusions.

English – Reading
Level 4: Pupils show understanding of significant ideas.
Level 5: Pupils show an understanding of a range of texts. They use different features of texts to obtain meaning.

English – Writing
Level 4: Pupils are beginning to use punctuation within the sentence.
Level 5: Pupils' writing is varied and interesting, conveying meaning clearly in a range of forms.

ICT
Level 4: Pupils can use ICT to research and find information. Pupils can use ICT to present their work.
Level 5: Pupils can develop and refine their work using desktop publishing.

Links to Literacy Framework

Year 5, Term 3

Word level work

W3 – use dictionaries and IT spell-checks.

Sentence level work

S4 – to use punctuation marks accurately in sentences.

Text level work

T2 – to identify the point of view from which a story is told.
T10 – to write discursively about a novel or story.
Revision of Term 2, T13 – to review and edit writing to produce a final form.

Assessment sheet

Name:_____ Date: _____

	Achieved	To achieve

Speaking and Listening:

Level 4:
• Talk is adapted to the purpose and he/she conveys his/her opinions clearly.

Level 5:
• Uses vocabulary that is appropriate to the purpose.
• Can collect ideas together, evaluate them and come to conclusions.

Reading:

Level 4:
• Shows understanding of significant ideas.

Level 5:
• Shows understanding of a range of texts.
• Uses different features of texts to obtain meaning.

Writing:

Level 4:
• Beginning to use punctuation within the sentence.

Level 5:
• Writing is varied and interesting, conveying meaning clearly in a range of forms.

ICT:

Level 4:
• Can use ICT to research and find information.
• Can use ICT to present their work.

Level 5:
• Can develop and refine their work for specific purposes.

Task sheet 1

Comparing science fiction texts

Aim

To identify the features of some science fiction texts and to compare their content.

Tasks

- Use the **My action planning sheet** to help you plan your work.

- **Read** the extracts through carefully.

- For each extract complete a **Story map sheet**. This will help you to understand how the stories are presented to the reader. Share your ideas with others in your group.

- For each extract **make a list** of all the scientific information that is included in the stories by completing the **Information sheet**.

- Finally, **choose one** of the extracts and write some paragraphs explaining the reasons why you think the extract is interesting.

  Think about:

    - the story;
    - the words used to describe the situation;
    - your responses to the story.

Task sheet 2

Writing a science fiction story

Aim

To write a science fiction story that shows how a scientific discovery may be used in the future.

Tasks

• Use the **My action planning sheet** to help you plan your work.

• **Discuss the text extracts** with others in your group. What scientific discoveries/ inventions did you find in them? (Your **Information sheet** from **Task sheet 1** will help you.)

• In pairs, **choose** a science fiction text (you may want to choose a story other than the text extracts) and explain to others in your group how the author has used a scientific idea to tell us about what the future may be like.

• **Read** the **Isaac Asimov sheet** to find out how this author uses scientific ideas in his writing.

• From your discussions, **make a list** of some of the scientific discoveries that have been used by science fiction writers. **Find out** about other scientific discoveries that scientists have recently made. Add these to your list. Use the **Resources sheet** to help you.

• **Choose** a scientific discovery from the list and use this idea to plan a science fiction story of your own that shows how this discovery may be used in the future. Use the **Science fiction story guide** to help you plan.

• Write and edit your story using a word processing program.

Extension work

• Imagine you are designing a classroom for the future. Draw a plan of it and explain what you would put in it and why.

Planning guidelines

What to do

1. Read the task sheets carefully then make up your action plan of tasks to do and when to do them by completing the 'My action planning sheet'. Ask your teacher to help you with anything you are not sure of.

2. When reading the extracts, make a note of anything you do not understand. Use these notes to ask your teacher for any help you might need. You may need to read the texts a couple of times to make sure you understand everything that is happening in them.

3. Completing the 'Story map' sheet will help you to understand what the stories are about and how the authors present their ideas to their readers.

4. To help you understand how authors have used scientific discoveries in their stories, you will need to complete the 'Information sheet' for each extract. After completing the sheet you may find that all the texts have certain things in common with each other. Some of these things will be common with other science fiction stories too.

5. Reading the 'Isaac Asimov' sheet will help you understand how one author has used scientific ideas in his work.

6. Before you plan your own science fiction story, use the 'Resources sheet' to help you develop ideas for your story.

7. The 'Science fiction story guide' will help you write your story. Think of how a scientific discovery might be developed and further used in the future. Make your ideas as fantastic as possible!

8. After you have planned your story, write it out using a suitable word processing program on the computer. Remember to save your story every time you complete a paragraph. Use pictures imported from scans or clip art to illustrate it.

9. Then share your story with someone in your group. Do they think you need to make any changes? Edit your story to improve it and then print out a final version.

Resources

Internet	www.scholastic.com/animorphs/books/animorphography www.scholastic.com/kaapplegate/about.htm www.lsi.usp.br/~rbianchi/clarke/acc.biography.html www.booksfactory.com/writers/asimov.htm www.frontiers4libraries.org.uk/science_clubs.asp	Try CD-Rom encyclopaedias
Speakers and other sources	Invite a scientist into school to tell you about new discoveries and how they will help people in the future.	Contact by writing or phoning – ask your teacher first.
Libraries	Your local library will have science fiction books you can borrow and read.	The librarian will help you.
Visits	Plan a visit to a science museum to look at the development of science over the years.	These can be individual or group visits. Discuss places to visit with friends.
Audience	Your audience is your group and teacher.	
Your own ideas	Discuss your ideas with your friends and teacher before you write your story. Will it be a believable story?	Discuss your ideas with friends and your teacher.

Story map

Science fiction

Setting

Where does the story take place?

When does the story take place?

Title and author:

_____

_____

Science fiction

Language

Who is telling the story?
– a narrator or the author?

Is the story written in the first person or the third person?

List some of the words the writer uses to describe where the story takes place.

Characters

Who are the main characters?

What are they like? Good? Bad?

What do they do in the story?

Do you like them?

Characters

List some of the words the writer uses to describe the characters.

The plot

List the facts the author uses in the story.

What sort of future does the story show?

Would you like to live in the time written about?

Information sheet

Science fiction

extract	scientific equipment mentioned	type of science mentioned (biology, chemistry, physics)	futuristic scientific information mentioned	important scientific facts (things that are true) that are mentioned
An Ape about the House				
The Sentinel				
Little Lost Robot				
Animorphs – the Illusion				

Science fiction story guide

Science fiction

Remember

Write your story using a word processing program – make sure you save your work after finishing each paragraph.

Check your spelling and punctuation.

Things to think about

Decide what scientific information you will use in the story - make a list of all the things you want to include.

Are your characters believable? Are they described as ordinary humans in a futuristic world?

Who will tell the story – a narrator or you as the author?

Make sure you brainstorm ideas for each part of the story.

My science fiction story

Features of science fiction stories

uses scientific and technical vocabulary

set in the future

often deals with problems people face in the future

fantastic settings

often uses time travel

uses detailed descriptions

human characters are usually rather ordinary

often includes encounters with aliens

space travel

Beginning

Set the scene for the reader.
Where is the story set?
What year is it?

Introduce the characters. Use adjectives to describe them.

Make the beginning exciting so that the reader wants to find out more.

Development

What happens to the characters?

What problems do they face?

Who do they turn to for help?

What fantastic scientific developments do they use?

Ending

Say how the problem was solved.

What happens to the characters in the end?

Text extract

from *Animorphs – The Illusion*
by K A Applegate

Ever since I overstayed the two-hour time limit in morph I've considered hawk to be my true form. Hawk is the body I have to keep if I want to help the other Animorphs and Ax combat the Yeerk invasion. Why was Rachel ignoring reality? She knew as well as anyone that I'd be out of the fight if I stayed more than two hours in human form.

All of which must sound strange. Possibly insane. So let me back up.

Here's the situation: the human race is under attack by a cruel and scheming enemy.

As you're reading this, the parasitic alien species called Yeerks continues to enslave human minds. Armed with a capability you can't even imagine till you've seen it in action, the Yeerks wrest from us the one thing we hold most dear: free will.

Once one of these slimy, grey, sluglike parasites squirms into your ear canal, and melds and shapes itself to all the crevices of your brain, it controls you. That's right. It dictates your every thought. Your every move! The Yeerks have created an army by infesting and controlling alien races.

Gedds. Taxxons. Hork-Bajir.

Humans.

By secretly infiltrating our society, the Yeerks have become a nearly undefeatable enemy. Who's fighting them? What's the human race's best and only hope in this war? A young Andalite cadet, along with five kids who call themselves the Animorphs because they alone, of all humans, possess a unique Andalite technology: the power to morph. To become any animal they can touch.

Ax, Jake, Cassie, Marco, Rachel. And me.

Together, we fight. But it can be a lonely war.

Because, see, morphing has some limitations.

And one involves a time limit. Stay in morph longer than two hours and you're stuck in morph for ever.

That's what happened to me. I was trapped as a red-tailed hawk. A nothlit, as the Andalites call someone stuck in morph.

(cont)

Text extract

from *Animorphs – The Illusion* by
KA Applegate (cont)

After many months, the powerful alien called the Ellimist gave me back my ability to morph. Even made it possible for me to morph into my former human body. I could choose to trap myself in my human form now, but I would lose my morphing power for good. Do you see? I would be useless. Unable to honour my responsibility to Earth, powerless to resist Yeerk evil.

"Just dance with me, Tobias. Please." A slow song started. I was surprised. I actually knew this one. Goo Goo Dolls. Couples filled up the dance floor. Cassie and Jake were on the other side of the gym, swaying gently, arms round each other.

Rachel reached out and took my hand.

It's funny. We've been on so many missions together. Battled Hork-Bajir-Controllers side by side. Saved each other's lives time and again. And still, after all that, it's something as simple as dancing that makes my heart pound.

Out on to the dance floor. I slid my arms around her waist. Felt her hands on my neck.

I let myself relax. Something I can rarely do as a hawk and an Animorph. I gave myself over to the moment. Let the music's rhythm lull me into a waking dream.

We danced, turning slowly. As we turned, my eyes wandered to the darkened scoreboard up in the corner. Banners listing the school's team victories. The seats, where a balloon had just broken free and sailed towards the ceiling.

And then I saw .... the clock.

Text extract

Science fiction

from *The Sentinel*
by Sir Arthur C Clarke

The next time you see the full Moon high in the south, look carefully at its right-hand edge and let your eye travel upward along the curve of the disk. Round about two o'clock you will notice a small, dark oval: anyone with normal eyesight can find it quite easily. It is the great walled plain, one of the finest on the Moon, known at the Mare Crisium – the Sea of Crises. Three hundred miles in diameter, and almost completely surrounded by a ring of magnificent mountains, it had never been explored until we entered it in the late summer of 1996.

Our expedition was a large one. We had two heavy freighters which had flown our supplies and equipment from the main lunar base in the Mare Serenitatis, five hundred miles away. There were also three small rockets which were intended for short-range transport over regions which our surface vehicles couldn't cross. Luckily, most of the Mare Crisium is very flat. There are none of the great crevasses so common and so dangerous elsewhere and very few craters or mountains of any size. As far as we could tell, our powerful caterpillar tractors would have no difficulty in taking us wherever we wished to go.

I was geologist – or selenologist, if you want to be pedantic – in charge of the group exploring the southern region of the Mare. We had crossed a hundred miles of it in a week, skirting the foothills of the mountains along the shore of what was once the ancient sea, some thousand million years before. When life was beginning on Earth, it was already dying here. The waters were retreating down the flanks of those stupendous cliffs, retreating into the empty heart of the Moon. Over the land which we were crossing, the tideless ocean had once been half a mile deep, and now the only trace of moisture was the hoar-frost one could sometimes find in caves which the searing sunlight never penetrated.

We had begun our journey early in the slow lunar dawn, and still had almost a week of Earth time before nightfall. Half a dozen times a day we would leave our vehicle and go outside in the space suits to hunt for interesting minerals, or to place markers for the guidance of future travellers. It was an uneventful routine. There is nothing hazardous or even particularly exciting about lunar exploration. We could live comfortably for a month in our

(cont)

60 Literacy
Challenges

Text extract

from *The Sentinel*
by Sir Arthur C Clarke (cont)

pressurized tractors, and if we ran into trouble we could always radio for help and sit tight until one of the spaceships came to our rescue.

We kept Earth time aboard the tractor, and precisely at 2200 hours the final radio message would be sent out to Base and we would close down for the day. Outside, the rocks would still be burning beneath the almost vertical Sun, but to us it was night until we awoke again eight hours later. Then one of us would prepare breakfast, there would be a great buzzing of electric razors, and someone would switch on the short-wave radio from Earth. Indeed, when the smell of frying sausages began to fill the cabin, it was sometimes hard to believe that we were not back on our own world – everything was so normal and homely, apart from the feeling of decreased weight and the unnatural slowness with which objects fell.

It was my turn to prepare breakfast in the corner of the main cabin that served as a galley. I can remember that moment quite vividly after all these years, for the radio had just played one of my favourite melodies, the old Welsh air 'David of the White Rock.' Our driver was already outside in his space suit, inspecting our caterpillar treads. My assistant, Louise Garnett, was up forward in the control position, making some belated entries in yesterday's log.

**from *A Taste of the Future*
by Arthur C Clarke**

An Ape About the House

Granny thought it a perfectly horrible idea; but then, she could remember the days when there were human servants.

"If you imagine," she snorted, "that I'll share the house with a monkey, you're very much mistaken."

"Don't be so old-fashioned," I answered. "Anyway, Dorcas isn't a monkey."

"Then what is she – it?"

I flipped through the pages of the Biological Engineering Corporation's guide. "Listen to this, Gran," I said. "'The Superchimp (Registered Trademark) Pan Sapiens is an intelligent anthropoid, derived by selective breeding and genetic modification from basic chimpanzee stock...'"

"Just what I said! A monkey!"

"'...and with a large-enough vocabulary to understand simple orders. It can be trained to perform all types of domestic work or routine manual labour and is docile, affectionate, housebroken, and particularly good with children...'"

"Children! Would you trust Johnnie and Susan with a – a gorilla?"

I put the handbook down with a sigh.

"You've got a point there. Dorcas is expensive, and if
I find the little monsters knocking her about..."

At this moment, fortunately, the door buzzer sounded. "Sign, please," said the delivery man. I signed, and Dorcas entered our lives.

"Hello, Dorcas," I said. "I hope you'll be happy here."

Her big, mournful eyes peered out at me from beneath their heavy ridges. I'd met much uglier humans, though she was rather an odd shape, being only about four feet tall and very nearly as wide. In her neat, plain uniform she looked just like a maid from one of those early twentieth-century movies; her feet, however, were bare and covered an astonishing amount of floor space.

(cont)

An Ape About the House (cont)

"Morning, Ma'am," she answered, in slurred but perfectly intelligible accents.

"She can speak!" squawked Granny.

"Of course," I answered. "She can pronounce over fifty words, and can understand two hundred. She'll learn more as she grows used to us, but for the moment we must stick to her vocabulary on pages forty-two and forty-three of the handbook." I passed, the instruction manual over to Granny; for once, she couldn't find even a single word to express her feelings.

Dorcas settled down very quickly. Her basic training – Class A Domestic, plus Nursery Duties – had been excellent, and by the end of the first month there were very few jobs around the house that she couldn't do, from laying the table to changing the children's clothes. At first she had an annoying habit of picking up things with her feet; it seemed as natural to her as using her hands, and it took a long time to break her of it. One of Granny's cigarette butts finally did the trick.

She was good-natured, conscientious, and didn't answer back.

Text extract

from *Little Lost Robot*
by Isaac Asimov

The general interrupted with a measure of authority. "I would like to explain that bit. I hadn't been aware that Dr. Calvin was unacquainted with the situation. I needn't tell you, Dr. Calvin, that there always has been strong opposition to robots on the Planet. The only defense the government has had against the Fundamentalist radicals in this matter was the fact that robots are always built with an unbreakable First Law – which makes it impossible for them to harm human beings under any circumstances.

"But we had to have robots of a different nature. So just a few of the NS-2 model, the Nestors, that is, were prepared with a modified First Law. To keep it quiet, all NS-2's are manufactured without serial numbers; modified members are delivered here along with a group of normal robots; and, of course, all our kind are under the strictest impressionment never to tell of their modification to unauthorized personnel." He wore an embarrassed smile. "This has all worked out against us now."

Calvin said grimly, "Have you asked each one who it is, anyhow? Certainly, you are authorized?"

The general nodded, "All sixty-three deny having worked here – and one is lying."

"Does the one you want show traces of wear? The others, I take it, are factory-fresh."

"The one in question only arrived last month. It, and the two that have just arrived, were to be the last we needed. There's no perceptible wear." He shook his head slowly and his eyes were haunted again. "Dr. Calvin, we don't dare let that ship leave. If the existence of non-First Law robots becomes general knowledge…" There seemed no way of avoiding understatement in the conclusion.

"Destroy all sixty-three," said the robopsychologist coldly and flatly, "and make an end of it."

Bogert drew back a corner of his mouth. "You mean destroy thirty thousand dollars per robot. I'm afraid U. S. Robots wouldn't like that. We'd better make an effort first, Susan, before we destroy anything."

"In that case," she said, sharply, "I need facts. Exactly what advantage does Hyper Base derive from these modified robots? What factor made them desirable, general?"

Kallner ruffled his forehead and stroked it with an upward gesture of his hand. "We had trouble with our previous robots. Our men work with hard radiations a good deal, you see.

(cont)

from *Little Lost Robot*
by Isaac Asimov (cont)

It's dangerous, of course, but reasonable precautions are taken. There have been only two accidents since we began and neither was fatal.

"However, it was impossible to explain that to an ordinary robot. The First Law states – I'll quote it – 'No robot may harm a human being, or through inaction, allow a human being to come to harm.'

"That's primary, Dr. Calvin. When it was necessary for one of our men to expose himself for a short period to a moderate gamma field, one that would have no physiological effects, the nearest robot would dash in to drag him out. If the field were exceedingly weak, it would succeed, and work could not continue till all robots were cleared out. If the field were a trifle stronger, the robot would never reach the technician concerned, since its positronic brain would collapse under gamma radiations – and then we would be out one expensive and hard-to-replace robot.

"We tried arguing with them. Their point was that a human being in a gamma field was endangering his life and that it didn't matter that he could remain there half an hour safely. Supposing, they would say, he forgot and remained an hour. They couldn't take chances. We pointed out that they were risking their lives on a wild off-chance. But self-preservation is only the Third Law of Robotics – and the First Law of human safety came first. We gave them orders; we ordered them strictly and harshly to remain out of gamma fields at whatever cost. But obedience is only the Second Law of Robotics – and the First Law of human safety came first. Dr. Calvin, we either had to do without robots, or do something about the First Law – and we made our choice."

"I can't believe," said Dr. Calvin, "that it was found possible to remove the First Law."

"It wasn't removed, it was modified," explained Kallner. "Positronic brains were constructed that contained the positive aspect only of the Law, which in them reads: 'No robot may harm a human being.' That is all. They have no compulsion to prevent one coming to harm through an extraneous agency such as gamma rays. I state the matter correctly, Dr. Bogert?"

"Quite," assented the mathematician.

"And that is the only difference of your robots from the ordinary NS-2 model? The only difference? Peter?"

"The only difference, Susan."

Isaac Asimov

Text extract from the introduction of *I Robot* by Isaac Asimov

Science fiction has certain satisfactions peculiar to itself. It is possible, in trying to portray future technology, to hit close to home. If you live long enough after writing a particular story, you may actually have the pleasure of finding your predictions reasonably accurate and yourself hailed as a sort of minor prophet.

This has happened to me in connection with my robot stories.

I began writing robot stories in 1939, when I was nineteen years old, and, from the first, I visualized them as machines, carefully built by engineers, with inherent safeguards, which I called 'The Three Laws of Robotics.' (In doing so, I was the very first to use the word 'robotics' in print, this taking place in the March, 1942 issue of *Astounding Science Fiction*.)

As it happened, robots of any kind were not really practical until the mid-1970's when the microchip came into use. Only that made it possible to produce computers that were small enough and cheap enough, while possessing the potentiality for sufficient capacity and versatility, to control a robot at nonprohibitive expense.

We now have machines, called robots, that are computer-controlled and are in industrial use. They increasingly perform simple and repetitious work on the assembly lines – welding, drilling, polishing and so on – and they are a recognized field of study and the precise word that I invented is used for it – robotics.

To be sure, we are only at the very beginning of the robotic revolution. The robots now in use are little more than computerized levers and are very far from having the complexity necessary for the Three Laws to be built into them. Nor are they anything close to human in shape, so they are not yet the 'mechanical men' that I have pictured in my stories, and that have appeared on the screen innumerable times.

Nevertheless, the direction of movement is clear. The primitive robots that have come into use are not the Frankenstein-monsters of equally primitive science fiction. They do not lust for human life (although accidents involving robots can result in human death, just as accidents with automobiles or electrical machinery can). They are, rather, carefully designed devices intended to relieve human beings of arduous, repetitive, dangerous, nonrewarding duties so that, in intent and in philosophy they represent the first steps toward my story-robots.

The steps that are yet to come are expected to proceed further in the direction I have marked out. A Number of different firms are working on 'home robots' that will have a vaguely human appearance and will fulfill some of the duties that once devolved on servants.

The results of all this is that I am held in considerable regard by those working in the field of robotics. In 1985, a fat encyclopedic volume entitled *Handbook of Industrial Robotics* (edited by Shimon Y. Nof and published by John Wiley) appeared, and, on request of the editor, I supplied it with an introduction.

Of course, in order to appreciate the accuracy of my predictions, I had to be fortunate enough to be a survivor. My first robots appeared in 1939, as I say, and I had to live for over forty more years in order to discover I was a prophet. Because I had begun at a very early age, and because I was fortunate, I managed to do this and words cannot tell you how grateful I am for that.

Fantasy worlds

Teacher's notes

Purposes

- To explore how authors use settings in fantasy stories.
- To apply geographical knowledge to creative writing.
- To interpret written information into a visual form.
- To develop thinking, planning and time management skills.

Aims

- To choose a setting from a fantasy story and make a visual and written representation of it.
- To write a description of a fantasy world and draw or make an accompanying visual representation of it.

Resources required

The pupil will need copies of the following:

1	'Challenge' sheet	page 143
2	'My action planning sheet'	page 144
3	'Task sheets'	pages 71 and 72
4	'Planning guidelines'	page 73
5	'Resources' sheet	page 74
6	'Comparison sheet'	page 75
7	'Story settings sheet'	page 76
8	'Geographical features chart'	page 77
9	'Description guide'	page 78
10	Text extracts	pages 79–84
11	'Skills sheets'	pages 145–148

The teacher's role

1 Introducing the challenge

Write the following into the top box of a copy of the 'Challenge' sheet (page 143):

You are going to read some text extracts about fantasy worlds. You are to choose one of these worlds and make a visual and written representation of it.

You are then going to invent your own fantasy world, write a detailed description of it and make a model or do a drawing of it.

Then photocopy the 'Challenge sheet' and give it to the pupils. Alternatively, they could be given a blank copy of the sheet and write the challenge on it themselves. It is important for them to have the challenge to refer to.

2 Providing support for the task sheets

Reading the texts

Before sharing the texts, discuss with the pupils what they already know about fantasy stories. Have they read any before? Do they like these types of stories? Why/why not? Do they know any well-known fantasy story authors? What is different about fantasy stories compared with other stories?

Explain that they will be reading three text extracts written by different authors: *Looking for Ilyriand* by Jay Ashton, *Mirror Dreams* by Catherine Webb and *Dance of the Midnight Fire* by Cormac MacRaois.

Have the pupils read any stories by these authors before? What do they know about these authors?

About the extracts

Mirror Dreams was written when the author was only 14. It has a sequel Mirror Wakes *(available from www.atombooks.co.uk). The book is about a land that keeps every dream and nightmare people have had. Usually these dreams and nightmares balance but there are those that want this balance to fail.*

Dance of the Midnight Fire is an adventure set in 'The Land of Dreaming'. Three children have to help the land survive and help its people drink from the magic waters of the Land of Youth. Evil stands in their way.

Looking for Ilyriand is a story about a quest. Six people, a goose, a dog and a dragon travel from their home to find Ilyriad – a lost country. The journey has its dangers and the group learn about each other and the importance of the environment on their journey.

The extracts could be shared with the class as a whole with everyone carrying out the activities on 'Task sheet 1'. The more able pupils should be able to carry out the work independently while the teacher leads the discussions with the rest of the class.

Questions that could be asked include:
- 'What is a story setting? Is the setting an important aspect of all stories – or in some genres more than others? Why?'
- 'How important is the setting in these extracts? Does the setting dominate in some texts more than others?'
- 'What information are we given in the first two paragraphs that help us to imagine the setting?'

Using the 'Comparison sheet'
This sheet enables the pupils to make comparisons between the text extracts. It is important to remind them to use word 'evidence' from the texts to answer the questions. Guide them when they consider the geographical features contained in the texts (clues as to what these could include are found on the 'Geographical features chart'). They may need reminding that geographical features include manufactured as well as natural physical features.

Organise the pupils into pairs for this task with different pairs working on different texts so their information can be shared at the end of the session.

Using the 'Story settings sheet'
This sheet enables the pupils to make a more detailed study of the settings in each text. Again, they are encouraged to use actual words from the texts as evidence. They could work in pairs using different extracts each and share their information at the end. They would all have access to this information if a summary of the discussion were to be displayed.

Completing both the 'Comparison sheet' and 'Story settings sheet' will provide the pupils with enough evidence to write their diary about 'visiting' one of the fantasy worlds. It will also help them to visualise the worlds more clearly in order to make their model, collage or painting.

It may be necessary to revise with the pupils what a diary entry would be like – how diaries are written, what their purpose is and how they might be set out.

Using the 'Geographical features chart'
This sheet will help the pupils to focus on the geographical features of their chosen fantasy worlds in order to stimulate ideas for inventing their own world. The teacher may need to explain what some of the geographical features are or encourage the pupils to find out for themselves.

Using the 'Description guide'
This guide will help the pupils plan and write their description of their invented fantasy world. The teacher needs to discuss each aspect of the guide with them before they start to make sure they understand what a descriptive piece of writing is.

A useful discussion would be to consider whether it would be possible to invent a fantasy world that doesn't have any 'real' geographical features found on our Earth. After all, most fantasy settings seem to have some aspects of our known world, such as plains, mountains, hills and water features. The challenge for the pupils is to invent a world that has these features but they are more fantastic or incredible than our own – a mountain that can move or plains made of rubber, for example! The writer needs to remember, however, that the reader must be able to believe in the world they describe for the story to work.

Encourage the pupils to be as creative as they can with their visual representation of their fantasy world. This aspect of the challenge also needs careful planning. What resources will they need? Are these readily available? How large should it be? Will it be best represented in two or three dimensions? How long will they take to make it?

Links to the National Curriculum

English – Speaking and Listening
Level 4: Pupils show understanding of significant ideas. Talk is adapted to the purpose of the task set.
Level 5: Pupils respond to others in discussion and make contributions that take into account others' views.

English – Reading
Level 4: The text is referred to when explaining views.
Level 5: Pupils identify key features and select words and phrases to support their views.

English – Writing
Level 4: Vocabulary choices are adventurous and words are used for effect.
Level 5: Vocabulary choices are imaginative and words are used precisely. Words with complex regular patterns are usually spelt correctly.

Geography
Level 4: Pupils can recognise and describe physical and human features.
Level 5: Pupils can describe the similarities and differences of different places.

Art and Design

Level 4: Pupils can explore ideas and select visual and other information.
Level 5: Pupils can explore ideas and assess visual and other information.

Links to Literacy Framework

Year 5, Term 3

Word level work
W3 – use dictionaries and IT spell-checks.

Sentence level work
S4 – to use punctuation marks accurately in sentences.

Text level work
T16 – to fillet passages for relevant information. Revision of Term 2
T13 – to review and edit writing to produce a final form.

Assessment sheet

Fantasy worlds

Name:_____ Date: _____

	Achieved	To achieve
Speaking and Listening:		
Level 4:		
• Shows understanding of significant ideas.		
• Talk is adapted to the purpose.		
Level 5:		
• Responds to others in discussion and makes contributions that take into account others' views.		
Reading:		
Level 4:		
• Text is referred to when explaining views.		
Level 5:		
• Can identify key features and select words and phrases to support their views.		
Writing:		
Level 4:		
• Vocabulary choices are adventurous and words are used for effect.		
Level 5:		
• Vocabulary choices are imaginative and words are used precisely.		
• Words with complex regular patterns are usually spelt correctly.		
Geography:		
Level 4:		
• Can recognise and describe physical and human features.		
Level 5:		
• Can describe the similarities and differences between places.		
Art and design:		
Level 4:		
• Can explore ideas and select visual and other information.		
Level 5:		
• Can explore ideas and assess visual and other information.		

Task sheet 1

Exploring settings in texts

Aim

To choose a setting from a fantasy story and make a visual and written representation of it.

Tasks

- Use the **My action planning sheet** to help you plan your work.

- **Read** the extracts through carefully.

- Complete the **Comparison sheet** to compare the three stories. Then **share** your responses with someone else in your group.

- Explore the settings of the stories in more detail by completing the **Story settings sheet**.

- **Choose one** of the extracts and do the following:

  - **draw/paint**, **make a model/collage** or **draw a map** of the fantasy world described in this extract. **Write down quotes** from the text that give you the evidence you need in order to do this.

  - pretend that you have visited this fantasy world. **Write a diary entry** about your visit there. Remember to write in the first person, using 'I'.

Think about:

  - what a diary is for (to record your activities, thoughts and ideas);

  - the purpose of this entry (to express your views about this fantasy world);

  - what you want to explain about this world (its features, characteristics and atmosphere).

Task sheet 2

Inventing a fantasy world

Aim

To invent your own fantasy world, write a detailed description of it and make a visual representation of it.

Tasks

- Use the **My action planning sheet** to help you plan your work.

- In pairs, **choose** a fantasy film and a fantasy story of your own choice. Together, discuss the features and characteristics of the settings of the worlds in the book and the film. Compare these settings with the geographical features of our real world. Could these fantasy worlds exist here on Earth? Use the **Geographical features chart** to record your answers. Report what you found out to the others in your group.

- **Invent** a fantasy world of your own. Think carefully about what this world might look like. Read different descriptions of fantasy worlds in books to help you decide how yours might look. Record the geographical features of your world on the **Geographical features chart**.

- **Write** a **detailed description** of your world. Use the **Description guide** to help you plan it. Use a word processing program to write and edit your description.

- Make a visual representation of your fantasy world. It could be a model, a drawing/painting or a collage.

Extension work

- Design a travel brochure for a fantasy world. It will be a safe world for holidaymakers. How will they get there and what will a family be able to enjoy on this holiday planet?

Planning guidelines

What to do

1. Read the task sheets carefully then make up your action plan of tasks to do and when to do them by completing the 'My action planning sheet'. Ask your teacher to help you with anything you are not sure of.

2. When reading the extracts, make a note of anything you do not understand. Use these notes to ask your teacher for any help you might need. You may need to read the texts a couple of times to make sure you understand everything that is happening in them.

3. Completing the 'Comparison sheet' will help you to compare the three extracts. Remember to use actual words from the texts to complete the sheet to remind you of the language the authors used.

4. Completing the 'Story settings sheet' enables you to consider the settings in more detail.

5. When you write your diary entry about visiting one of the worlds in the text extracts, remember to write in the first person and use the word 'I'.

6. When you are comparing a fantasy book and a fantasy film, remember that you are thinking about whether or not the geographical features of these worlds are like our real world. You may need to want to use information books or the internet to find unusual geographical features that you include in your own fantasy world. Remember to ask your teacher's permission first.

7. Be as creative as you dare when you invent your own fantasy world! Read lots of descriptions from fantasy stories to help you decide what your world might look like.

8. The 'Description guide' will help you write your description of your world.

9. After you have planned your description, write it out using a suitable word processing program on the computer. Remember to save your story every time you complete a paragraph.

10. Then share your story with someone in your group. Do they think you need to make any changes? Edit your description to improve it and then print out a final version.

11. Think carefully about how you will visually represent your fantasy world – will a model or a drawing be best?

Resources

Internet	www.bbc.co.uk/learning/library/physical_geography.shtml	Try CD-Rom encyclopaedias
	www.enchantedlearning.com/geography/landforms.shtml	
	Catherine Webb – www.atombooks.co.uk	
	book blurb – *Dance of the Midnight Fire* – www.clarelibrary.ie/eolas/library/services/book-promos/children/midnight.htm	
Speakers and other sources	A local artist who draws landscapes may be able to help you with ideas and techniques.	Contact by writing or phoning – ask your teacher first.
	Model makers may be able to help you with ideas. Contact your local model making society.	
	Landscape gardeners may be able to tell you how plants grow in particular climates.	
Libraries	A visit to the library to find Fantasy books and a talk from the librarian will be useful. The librarian could also visit school with books that would be useful.	The librarian will help you.
Visits	Visits to exotic gardens and museums could prove to be useful sources of ideas for your work.	These can be individual or group visits. Discuss places to visit with friends.
Audience	Your audience is your group, teacher and year group.	
Your own ideas	Discuss your ideas for your work with your friends and teacher.	Discuss your ideas with friends and your teacher.

Fantasy worlds

Comparison sheet

extract	Where is the story set? How do you know? (use words from the text)	What sort of people are in the story? (use words from the text)	What are the geographical features? (use words from the text)	What is the mood of the place like? (use words from the text)
Looking for Ilyriand				
Mirror Dreams				
Dance of the Midnight Fire				

Story settings sheet
Fantasy worlds

extract	What type of place is the story set in? (use words from the text)	Is the place: friendly or hostile, busy or quiet? magical? or something else?	What kinds of buildings are there? (use words from the text)	What other features stand out? (use words from the text)
Looking for Ilyriand				
Mirror Dreams				
Dance of the Midnight Fire				

Geographical features chart

Fantasy worlds

Does it have this feature?	Name of fantasy world from a book	Name of fantasy world from a film	Name of my fantasy world
mountains			
hills			
valleys			
plains/ grasslands			
volcanoes			
cliffs			
caves			
beaches			
islands			
deserts			
rivers			
lakes			
seas/ oceans			
other water			
stones			
forests			
roads			
buildings			
towns/ cities			
weather conditions			
other (list them)			

Description guide

Fantasy worlds

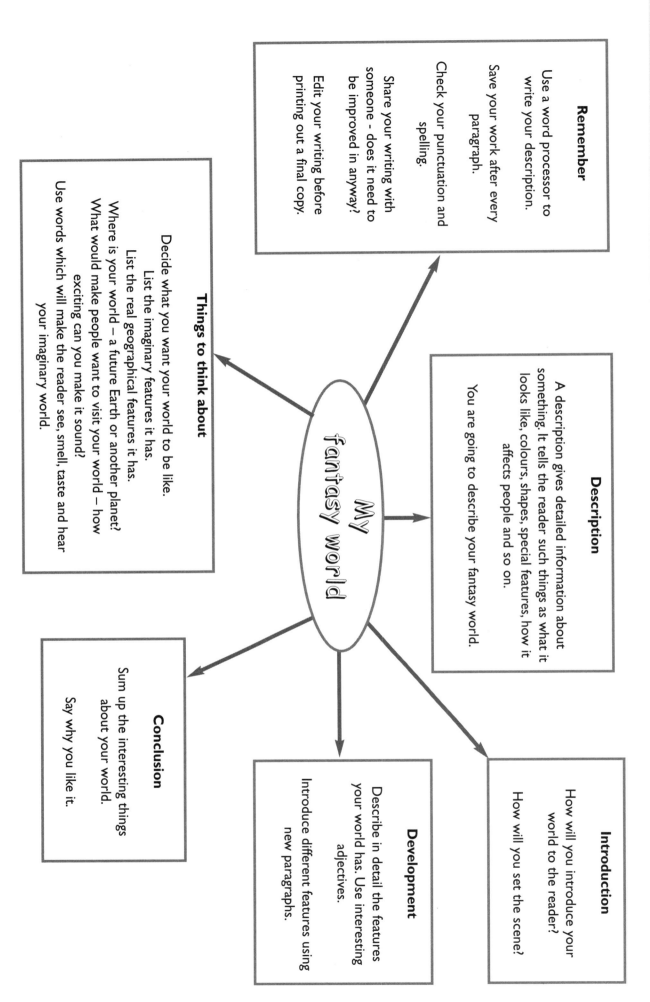

Remember

Use a word processor to write your description.

Save your work after every paragraph.

Check your punctuation and spelling.

Share your writing with someone - does it need to be improved in anyway?

Edit your writing before printing out a final copy.

Description

A description gives detailed information about something. It tells the reader such things as what it looks like, colours, shapes, special features, how it affects people and so on.

You are going to describe your fantasy world.

My fantasy world

Things to think about

Decide what you want your world to be like.

List the imaginary features it has.

List the real geographical features it has.

Where is your world – a future Earth or another planet?

What would make people want to visit your world – how exciting can you make it sound?

Use words which will make the reader see, smell, taste and hear your imaginary world.

Introduction

How will you introduce your world to the reader?

How will you set the scene?

Development

Describe in detail the features your world has. Use interesting adjectives.

Introduce different features using new paragraphs.

Conclusion

Sum up the interesting things about your world.

Say why you like it.

Text extract

from *Looking for Ilyriand*
by Jay Ashton

They went down towards the town, eager and curious, except for Conrad, who was tight-lipped and angry – angry that he had been disobeyed, still more because he had been proved wrong. Unable to give vent to his fury, he smarted and glared unforgivingly about.

The town was at the meeting of three roads and a river and already, early in the morning of another hot day, brimmed with activity. There was so much noise, of men and of animals, that at first they could make little sense of the scene. They were constantly buffeted by the crowds, and their attention pulled this way and that by shouts and clangs and flashes of colour.

Trees grew along the main street; in their shade sheets were laid out and on them goods arranged. Strange vegetables and curious fruits in small neat piles; heaps of mysterious gold and orange titbits, enticingly scented; cooking pots; the long hooded robes which seemed to be the local dress; leather shoes and harnesses; knives with handles intricately worked and glinting in the sun. A man yoked to a pair of urns poured cups of some pale frothy liquid. Another juggled with shiny skittles, and another played a pipe. Several small boys gathered round the travellers, pulling at their clothes, shouting at them, holding out their hands. Receiving nothing, they continued to follow, shouting what sounded like abuse. In the general din the Fallonders hardly noticed. Everywhere animals bleated and bellowed and whined, while people called, gesticulated, offered, begged, haggled. It was all very tempting, but they had nothing to barter.

Eventually they stopped by a well, hoping to get at least a drink of water without payment. Then Derwin, who held Emma firmly clasped under one arm, was accosted by a man in a brown robe. The man held out some pieces of copper and pointed at the goose. Derwin shook his head. The man groped in his robe and produced more copper, holding it out with one hand and pulling at the goose with the other. Emma pecked the man, Derwin clutched her to his chest and turned away. The man went off, yelling angrily.

"Why turn down a good offer?" enquired Ferdy maliciously.

Derwin, looking worried, called Kerrin to his side.

(cont)

from *Looking for Ilyriand*
by Jay Ashton (cont)

"Look at that!" cried Mirim, pointing to a boy who, with many flourishes, was thrusting flaming torches into his mouth.

Prothero snorted. "That's nothing! I could do better than that when I was still the egg." He threw back his head and belched out a great gout of blue flame.

The effect on the bystanders was astonishing. As one, they threw themselves on their faces and covered their heads with their arms. Prothero, his flame dwindling, stared at them incredulously. "Well!" he exclaimed. "At last a really appreciative audience."

"You should not be doing this," said a voice severely. Derwin turned and saw a thin, bearded man and behind him, smiling and bobbing, his friend the drummer.

"I am Cassian," said the bearded man. "I am cousin of him. I am poet. I am speaking well your language. Is good?" His eyes swept over the group and fell on Conrad. "To you, Esteemed Leader, I am bidding – welcome!" With an elaborate flourish he bowed to the ground before Conrad.

Conrad looked wonderingly at Cassian. The foreigner wore a white, embroidered robe, its hood thrown back to reveal luxuriant black curls, glossy cheeks, and melting brown eyes. Awkwardly Conrad nodded back.

"Most respected travellers," Cassian went on, with eloquent waves of his arms. "Not only –" he bowed to Derwin, " – a most accomplished musician, but also a great dragon beast of magic powers!"

"What do you mean, magic powers?" demanded Prothero, suspecting sarcasm.

"The sacred blue flame. O Magnificent One! None may be looking on it save they of blood royal!"

"Sounds like a lot of rot to me," said Ronan.

Text extract

from *Dance of the Midnight Fire*
by Cormac MacRaois

"Look!" she whispered, pointing.

Beyond the outer ring of fire stood a tall pale figure with flowing white hair and beard. Even as they looked at him he faded so that they could see right through him to the fields beyond. Then his image grew clearer again.

"Is that your ghost?" asked Daire.

"Yes," replied Niamh.

"He's coming this way!" cried Rónán.

They watched in fear and wonder as the figure drifted towards them. He moved through the fire as if it wasn't there, keeping his eyes fixed on them. As he drew nearer he seemed to grow larger and more powerful. The children huddled together, clinging to each other.

Suddenly the nearest ring of fire rushed forward towards the Cairn. The children leaped back against the great stone. There was a blinding flash of light. A thunderclap shook the earth and air. The Cairn seemed to swing upside-down and the children were falling, spinning dizzily through blackness while circles of fire flickered all around them. After a time they began to fall more slowly.

The fires grew blurred, then melted away. At last they felt something beneath their feet, though even then they didn't feel sure that they weren't still falling. They stood, breathing heavily, holding on to each other, not daring to move.

"What happened?" whispered Rónán.

"We must have fallen off the earth or through the sky," replied Daire.

They listened. There was no sound.

"I wonder where we are?" said Niamh." There's grass here and lots of stones too."

It was quite dark but far off they could see a glimmer of pale light. As they watched, it grew brighter. Now they could see the dark outline of distant hills, then some odd shapes nearer to them. The light grew brighter still. Somewhere a bird chirped. A long ray of light flickered across the countryside from the bottom of the sky and a bright sun peeped silently over the rim of the world.

The children looked around them. They were standing on a low hill. The odd shapes they had noticed earlier

from *Dance of the Midnight Fire*
by Cormac MacRaois (cont)

were the ruins of hundreds of buildings. Beyond the ruins a wide grassy plain stretched for miles to a line of misty blue hills on the horizon.

Directly behind the children there was an enormous white dolmen. The paved area where they were standing was surrounded by three circles of standing stones. Four wide avenues ran out from the dolmen to the east, west, north and south. Along the eastern avenue a tall man in flowing robes was walking towards them with powerful strides.

"It's the ghost!" whispered Daire.

He no longer looked shadowy or grey. His hair and beard were golden and he looked strong and solid. His long robes glistened with a thousand colours reflected from the sunlight. He strode right up to the edge of the inner circle. Then he stopped, bowed courteously and said, "You are welcome to Tír Danann, though I must apologise for the way in which you were brought here." His voice was strong and rich with a peculiar attractive accent as if he were used to speaking a different language. "I had to be sure you would come," he continued. "If I'd spoken to you in your own world you might not have trusted me as I believe we look

rather ghostly when we show ourselves in other worlds."

The children looked at each other.

"Have we been kidnapped?" asked Rónán.

"Oh no! Perhaps you could say that I borrowed you, but you may return to your own world anytime you want to."

"I think you should tell us who you are and why you have brought us here," said Niamh.

The stranger smiled at her. "Of course," he said. "I shall explain everything if you will follow me."

He turned and began to walk back along the eastern avenue. The children followed a little distance behind him. The sun was now higher, its clear light brightening the empty street of the ruined city. The tall stranger walked so quickly that the children found it difficult to keep up with him.

"If he disappears among these ruins we'll be stuck here forever," muttered Daire as they hurried over the cracked paving stones and pieces of fallen pillars and arches. This had clearly been a great city a long time ago.

Text extract

from *Mirror Dreams*
by Catherine Webb

It doesn't matter, though. I know where the road leads. Through a hundred crossroads where possible destinies intersect – more than can ever be counted – the road will eventually lead back to Haven. All roads lead to Haven. Or away, depending on your point of view.

Unless you take the wrong turn, that is. Unless you follow the roads through shadier kingdoms. Unless you head west into the setting sun. Then you find Nightkeep, the other ancient kingdom, opposed in every way to its twin. You'd be amazed how many idiots can't tell shadow from light and accidentally wander into that realm of dark magic and confusion.

Think of it as a family tree. At the top are two brothers. Haven and Nightkeep. They have children – the kingdoms – which spread out quickly into the Void as more and more mages build more and more lands to call their own. Until there are now two quite definite families, glowering at each other over an infinite expanse of nothingness.

And there you have it. Haven and Nightkeep.

My little Stormpoint is on the far edge of the network of roads leading from Haven. Many mages have come here, asking if they might build their own kingdoms beyond mine, but rather than delight in the tax I could then raise from their visitors, I turn them away. I do not like the thought of two roads to watch. Just one inbound lane is good enough for me.

This stubbornness puts me eight kingdoms away from Haven, the centre of the web. That is assuming I don't get horribly lost on the road, and the eight kingdoms between me and Haven don't think, 'Let's see if we can kill this mage and take Stormpoint while he is vulnerable and passing through our lands.'

Eight is a long way out, and it makes my position in the great social network of who-bosses-whom a rather low one.

But it doesn't matter. I have been to Earth, and beyond. I have seen Nightkeep, I have fought beside kings. No one will bully me for a good while yet.

(cont)

from *Mirror Dreams*
by Catherine Webb (cont)

Earth. The big granddaddy of them all, lurking even higher up the family tree than Haven and Nightkeep. The one source from which all this mess stems. The place where the light kingdoms of Haven meet the dark ones at Nightkeep. The place where the dreamers – the insubstantial shadows who make the Void in their sleep – come from. So the theory runs.

I have visited that strange place, and studied it well. It's a madhouse. Somewhere so strange and unexplainable must surely be real, for I do not believe human imagination alone could conjure up such horrors and such beauty, mingled together in such terrible and wondrous detail.

Don't you dare fall asleep on me yet!

The Void is not just an empty space – it is the nothingness of sleep, made by all these humans' dreamless nights on Earth. Either that or a natural phenomenon depending on where you stand in the academic wars that wage over this issue.

But this I can say with confidence, for I have seen it with my own eyes: Haven is not just a city – it is the city of dreams, the culmination of all those dreamers' wishes and desires. It is the golden city – heaven, if you will – where everyone wishes to be.

Philosophy

Teacher's notes

Purposes

- To explore the meaning of the terms 'philosophy', and 'ethics' in particular.

- To find out about the philosopher, Socrates.

- To think about and discuss issues in depth from a philosophical point of view.

- To develop thinking, planning and time management skills.

Aims

- To find out about philosophy and Socrates.

- To explore questions of ethics and write a set of agreed ethical rules for the class.

Resources required

The pupil will need copies of the following:

1	'Challenge sheet'	page 143
2	'My action planning sheet'	page 144
3	'Task sheets'	pages 88 and 89
4	'Planning guidelines'	page 90
5	'Resources' sheet	page 91
6	'Discussion sheet'	page 92
7	'Making rules guide'	page 93
8	Text extracts	pages 94–99
9	'Skills sheets'	page 145–148

The teacher's role

1 Introducing the challenge

Write the following into the top box of a copy of the 'Challenge' sheet (page 143):

You are going to read some text extracts about philosophy and a man called Socrates.

You are then going to work in a small group to explore questions of ethics in order to agree a set of class rules.

Then photocopy the 'Challenge sheet' and give it to the pupils. Alternatively, they could be given a blank copy of the sheet and write the challenge on it themselves. It is important for them to have the challenge to refer to.

2 Providing support for the task sheets

Reading the texts
Before sharing the texts, explain to the pupils that they are going to carry out some activities where a lot of group discussion is involved. You may want to remind them about criteria for successful group discussions, such as listening carefully to what others have to say, waiting your turn, accepting that others can have different and equally valid points of view and so on.

Read the extracts, with the pupils following the text as you read them. Begin with the text on philosophy, followed by the one about Socrates. This may be the first time that any of the pupils have had to consider such a challenging concept as philosophy so it is important that initially you lead the discussion.

Using the 'Discussion sheet'
This sheet can be used to guide the group discussion about the selected scenario and will enable them to make notes about any decisions made. It is important that the pupils discuss the definitions of terms mentioned in the scenarios. For example, they may well find that there are different opinions about what the term 'stealing' means. Does picking a flower from someone else's garden count as stealing, for example? The group should be asked for their comments on any issues that arise.

Using the 'Making rules guide'
This guide will direct the pupils' thoughts when deciding about their agreed set of rules. It outlines the kinds of questions they should ask themselves and gives guidelines for the purposes and functions of rules.

3 Other points to note

You may decide that all the activities on 'Task sheet 1' are best carried out with the whole class rather than asking the more able pupils to work in small groups.

Questions that could be asked include:

- 'Have you heard about philosophy or Socrates before? What did you already know?'
- 'Does the extract about Philosophy give you a good idea of what Philosophy is about?'

Socrates introduced questioning as a means of deepening thinking and the last activity on 'Task sheet 1' enables the pupils to explore this deeper thinking about things. Begin the discussion by asking what the pupils think 'know thyself' means. Have they ever stopped and thought about what kind of person they really are? What might be the important questions to ask if you are trying to learn more about yourself?

You should decide which scenario the group considers. The more able pupils could work in small groups on one scenario while you work with the rest of the class on another. A general discussion about why we have rules in our society would be beneficial – beginning perhaps with the class or school rules.

The agreeing of a set of rules could be developed as a whole class discussion and the agreed rules practised for a few weeks to see how valuable/effective they were. The discussion will work more effectively if the class sit in a circle.

Some pupils may not see the need for a set of values or rules, others will. They need careful guiding through what could potentially be threatening discussions for some.

NOTE: Useful websites for teachers:
http://socrates.clarke.edu/aplg0260.htm
http://socrates.clarke.edu/aplg0100.htm
www.historyforkids.org/teachers/guides/philosophy.htm
www.socratesway.com/weblinks.html

Links to the National Curriculum

English – Speaking and Listening

Level 4: Pupils talk and listen confidently.
Pupils show understanding of the main points.
Level 5: Pupils develop ideas thoughtfully.
He/she makes contributions that take account of others' views.
Standard English is used in formal situations.

English – Reading

Level 4: He/she shows understanding of significant ideas.
He/she uses the text when explaining his/her views.
Level 5: Pupils use inference and deduction where possible.
He/she identifies key features and shows understanding of words and phrases in the text.

English –Writing

Level 4: Writing is in a range of forms and is developed in interesting ways.
Spelling and punctuation is generally accurate.
Level 5: Meaning is conveyed in an appropriate form.
Words are used precisely.

PHSE:
Key Stage 2
Pupils show the ability to talk and write about their opinions.
Pupils can explain their views on a subject.
Pupils show understanding of why and how rules can be made and enforced.
Pupils show understanding of the consequences of bullying, lying, stealing.
Pupils appreciate the different responsibilities they have in the school community.
Pupils realise the nature and consequences of issues raised in the scenarios and offers solutions.

Links to Literacy Framework

Year 5, Term 1

Word level work
W3 – use dictionaries and IT spell-checks.

Sentence level work
S4 – to adapt writing for different readers and purposes.

Text level work
T26 – make notes for different purposes.

Assessment sheet

Name: _____ Date: _____

	Achieved	To achieve
Speaking and Listening:		

Speaking and Listening:

Level 4:
• Talks and listens confidently.
• Shows understanding of the main points.

Level 5:
• Develops ideas thoughtfully.
• Makes contributions that take account of others' views.
• Uses Standard English in formal situations.

Reading:

Level 4:
• Shows understanding of significant ideas
• Uses the text when explaining his/her views.

Level 5:
• Uses inference and deduction where appropriate.
• Identifies key features and shows understanding of words and phrases in the text.

Writing:

Level 4:
• Can write in a range of forms and writing is developed in interesting ways.
• Spelling and punctuation is generally accurate.

Level 5:
• Meaning is conveyed in an appropriate form.

PSHE:

Key Stage 2:
• Shows the ability to talk and write about his/her opinions.
• Can explain his/her views on a subject.
• Shows understanding of why and how rules can be made and enforced.
• Shows understanding of the consequences of bullying, lying, stealing to others.
• Appreciates the different responsibilities he/she has in the school community.
• Realises the nature and consequences of issues and can offer solutions.

Task sheet 1

Finding out about philosophy

Aim

To find out about philosophy and Socrates.

Tasks

- Use the **My action planning sheet** to help you plan your work.

- **Read** the **extracts** through carefully with your teacher.

- In the **philosophy extract**, we are told what philosophy is. **Write** down what you think philosophy means, using the information at the beginning of the extract. Share your ideas with your teacher and others.

- The study of philosophy is divided into four different areas:

  Metaphysics   Aesthetics   Ethics   Logic

  In groups, **write** down what you think each term means. Use the philosophy extract to help you. Then use a dictionary to check your definitions.

- In the **extract about Socrates** we are told he had a guiding rule. With a partner, decide:

  - What it was;

  - What you think it meant.

- What method did Socrates use to help his students learn the truth? Use the text extract and the **Resources** sheet to help you.

- **Discuss** with others how people might begin to 'know thyself'.

  - What do you think 'know thyself' means?

  - **Write** down the questions you think you could ask if you were trying to find out what sort of person you are.

Task sheet 2

Writing a set of rules

Aim

To discuss and write, as a group, an agreed set of class rules that show the use of ethics.

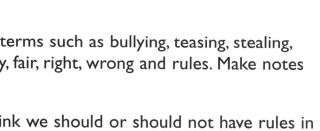

Tasks

- Use the **My action planning sheet** to help you plan your work.

- In a group, **read and discuss** the scenario your teacher gives you.

- **Read** the **questions** at the bottom of the scenario. **Decide** how you would answer them. **Write** down your ideas in note form on the **Discussion sheet**. **Share** your responses with others in your group. The **Rules guide** will help you with the last question on your scenario. Share your ideas with another group – do they think your rules will work?

- Use a **dictionary** to help you define terms such as bullying, teasing, stealing, responsibility, environment, community, fair, right, wrong and rules. Make notes on what you find out.

- With your group **discuss** why you think we should or should not have rules in our society. **Discuss and agree** a set of rules that you think your class could follow. Write them down and present them to the class. Use the **Rules guide** to help you.

Extension work

- Write to your teacher explaining why the rules you have chosen will be helpful to the class.

Planning guidelines Philosophy

What to do

1. Read the task sheets carefully then make up your action plan of tasks to do and when to do them by completing the 'My action planning sheet'. Ask your teacher to help you with anything you are not sure of.

2. When reading the extracts, make a note of anything you do not understand. Use these notes to ask your teacher for any help you might need.

   Underline any important words and explanations in the text. This will help you with 'Task sheet 1'.

   Use a dictionary to help you with the meaning of any words you do not understand.

3. Use the 'Resources sheet' to help you find out more about Socrates and his ideas. Remember to ask your teacher's permission before you contact anyone or use the internet.

4. In your discussion about the meaning of 'know thyself', make a list of questions you might want to think about. Decide what are the important questions to ask when you are trying to learn to 'know' yourself. One might be 'How do I see myself?'

5. For the activities in 'Task sheet 2', use the 'Resources sheet' to help you plan talks and visits in advance.

6. Use the 'Discussion sheet' to help you record your ideas about your group's scenario. Record your group's agreed rules.

   Remember to use a dictionary to look up the definitions of any terms relevant to your scenario. Different people may have different definitions of some terms.

7. Decide how you want to present your group's rules. Will you use words or words and illustrations? Use the 'Making rules guide' to help you.

8. Follow your rules for a couple of weeks. Do you think they were helpful? Will you keep them? Do any need changing?

90 **Literacy**
Challenges

Resources

Internet	Useful sites for pupils: www.woodlands-junior.Kent.sch.uk/Homework/Greece.html www.historyforkids.org/learn/philosophy/index.htm	Try CD Rom encyclopaedias
Speakers and other sources	The local clergy (multi-cultural) could be invited into school to discuss with the groups the ethics the scenarios raise. The local police liaison officer could discuss the problems that are caused when people break the law. A local lawyer could discuss the need for rules. The school site manager who can discuss the environment problems schools have. Amnesty International has information for schools about justice and fairness.	Contact by writing or phoning – ask your teacher first.
Libraries	The 'Children's Britannica' and other reference texts would provide information about Socrates and Philosophy.	The librarian will help you.
Visits	You could visit the law courts, police station to see how rules/laws are upheld.	These can be individual or group visits. Discuss places to visit with friends.
Audience	Your group, class, teacher and visitors.	
Your own ideas	Discuss your ideas with your teacher and your group. How can you carry out the tasks successfully?	Discuss your ideas with friends and your teacher.

Discussion sheet

Philosophy

What are the main points to consider in the scenario? List them here.

Write down the meanings/definitions of any key words in the scenario. For example, lies are…

Make notes here on your ideas for rules that would apply to your scenario and general rules for your class.

Write down the list of rules your group agreed on.

Making rules guide

Making rules

The scenario

What sort of rules does the scenario make you think about?

Make a list of them.

Rules

Rules are a set of guidelines that provide a code of conduct to be followed.

You are going to write a set of rules for your class.

Your class

What sort of rules do you think should apply to your classroom?

Make a list of them.

Think about things to do with safety, responsibility and thoughtfulness.

Things to think about

Why do we have rules in our society? Do we need them?
What rights and responsibilities do we all share?
Should we always be responsible for our own behaviour?
Should we concern ourselves with the behaviour of others?
Should there be different rules for adults and children?
Can rules make us feel happy and safe?
What should happen to people who break the rules?
What would life be like without any rules?
Do you know any rules that seem silly or unfair?
Is there such a thing as right and wrong?

Your rules

Are your rules fair?

Will people agree to them?

How can you help people to keep them?

What happens if they do not keep the rules?

Presenting your rules

How will you present your rules?

Will you use words only or words and pictures?

Where would be the best place to display your rules?

How will you explain them to make sure others understand what they mean?

Text extract

from *Children's Britannica*

PHILOSOPHY The word "philosophy" comes from two Greek words meaning "wisdom" and "love". The Greek Pythagoras, when asked if he were a wise man, replied, "No, but I am a lover of wisdom." By philosophy we mean man's efforts to understand his experiences and the world in which he lives.

Philosophy began with the first attempts of primitive man to understand the world – to discover what the heavenly bodies were, what caused plants to grow, what happened to men after their bodies died, and whether good or evil powers were in control of events.

Various philosophies have developed in Persia, India, China and in other eastern countries. But western philosophy is generally accepted to have begun in ancient Greece. Many of our modern beliefs about human rights and freedoms come from the teachings of Greek philosophers such as Aristotle, Plato and Socrates. The Greeks were interested in all areas of knowledge, including those that we now call "sciences". However, they based their conclusions on observation and reason, rather than on the results of experiments.

During the Middle Ages some philosophers worked to show that the ideas of Christianity were reasonable. Some Christian philosophers absorbed the thoughts of Aristotle. Others, particularly during the Renaissance, were critical of religion.

Philosophy is divided into various branches. For example, metaphysics is concerned with the nature of reality, aesthetics with the nature of art and beauty, and ethics with the study of right and good in human behaviour. Logic is the study of accurate thinking. The first great teacher of logic was Aristotle. Each school of philosophy has its own way of thinking and certain basic ideas. But each has the same goal – to establish what is true and valuable in man and the universe. That is why the philosopher keeps on testing the truth of statements other people make.

The way the philosopher thinks about things is really as important as what he thinks about. Whereas the mathematician, the scientist, the historian, and the ordinary man in the street take certain facts and rules of life for granted, the philosopher does not and often questions what others think as obvious.

Philosophy (cont)

For example, anyone looking along a railway track will say without hesitation that the two lines are parallel, but the philosopher will ask how he knows this when they do not look parallel. The further away the lines stretch, the closer together they appear to be. Of course we know from experience that the lines are always the same distance apart. But the philosopher asks us to think very carefully about why we believe this to be true, and in doing so helps us to guard against reaching the wrong answer in other cases which appear obvious, but in which the evidence may be misleading.

The philosopher might go on to ask a more important second question: "Why does the train run along the railway track?" The ordinary person might say that it was because people want to reach the other end. The scientist might explain how an engine works, and perhaps the historian would begin to describe how the first railway engine came to be built. But the philosopher is more likely to want to know why a particular train moves along the track. The question makes us think carefully about the causes of events in the world around us. This relationship is often referred to as cause and effect. The philosopher may also want to know what caused the "cause". He may also look carefully at causes and effects to see if there are any "gaps" between them; that

is, instances of "causes" not leading directly to effects. What the philosopher is really doing is making people think about the world around them, and making them realise how much they accept without question.

The third kind of question the philosopher asks is more important still and perhaps easier to understand. To return to the railway, if someone witnesses an accident he finds himself faced with a number of alternative courses of action, such as trying to help the injured or perhaps telephoning his family to tell them what has happened. When he is asked why he chooses to do one thing rather than another, he might say, "Because this is the right thing to do in the circumstances." Then the philosopher asks the same sort of question as before: "What do you mean by right? Do you mean what I ought to do or what a good man would do, or what will bring the most happiness to other people, or what?"

In all these examples the philosopher is trying to go a stage further back to find out what lies behind the words and ideas about things and actions. He believes that the truth itself is important for its own sake, whatever consequences it may have.

Text extract

from *Children's Britannica*

SOCRATES (c.470-399BC) was one of the greatest Greek philosophers. Little is known about Socrates' early life except that he served several times as a soldier and showed great bravery. He was born in Athens when that city was the leader of the world in literature, art and government.

Socrates knew all the most famous writers and statesmen of his time, but he had no desire to be famous himself. He only wanted to show people how to live wisely and happily, and to convince them that wisdom and honesty are more important than riches or fame. His guiding rule was "know thyself".

The young men of Athens were eager to learn from him. Socrates did not write down his teachings or invent any system of philosophy. Instead he talked with the young men wherever he met them, and started them thinking for themselves about what is good in life. Some of these young men later became writers and wrote down Socrates' ideas. The most important of his followers was Plato. Plato's writings are Dialogues in which the main speaker is Socrates, discussing some question with his young friends. Socrates would ask one of them to give an opinion on a subject. Socrates would then ask him questions. Often the person questioned had not really thought very deeply and had no good reason for his opinion. Then by more questioning they all tried to find the true answer. This method of learning the truth by asking questions has been named "Socratic" or "dialectic".

Once, someone asked the Oracle at Delphi "Who is the wisest man in Greece?" and the Oracle replied that it was Socrates. Socrates was astonished at this for he said that he asked questions because he himself did not know the answers. He began to talk to other men who were supposed to be wise. He discovered that they were only pretending to have wisdom. Thus Socrates found that he was the wisest because he alone knew his own ignorance.

Socrates made many enemies, and finally some of them brought him to trial in court. They accused him of being wrong in what he taught the young Athenians and of being disrespectful towards the gods. Socrates would not promise to stop his way of teaching. He said the he had done only good, and should be rewarded rather than punished. This made the jurors angry, and he was condemned to die by drinking hemlock, a slow but deadly poison. In his prison cell, while he was waiting for the poison to take effect, Socrates talked calmly with his friends about the new and better life of the soul after death.

Scenarios

Scenario 1

You are walking in the school corridor with a friend. You see another friend taking some crisps out of a lunch box that is not theirs. Your friend does not have much to eat at lunch times and is always hungry. Your friend walks away with the crisps. The owner of the lunch box arrives and discovers his crisps are missing. What do you think you should do?

- Is your friend stealing?
- How do you define stealing?
- Is it wrong to steal?
- Should you tell the teacher?
- Should you let your friend steal?
- How do you help the person who has had their crisps stolen?
- How do you help your friend to see that what has been done is wrong?
- What rules could your group have about respecting the belongings of others?
- How could your group see that they are carried out?

Scenario 2

One of your friends has not got enough money to buy his sister a birthday present. When you are walking to school with him, you see a five pound note in the playground. Your friend picks it up and puts it in his pocket. You carry on walking and a lady stops you and asks if you have seen a five pound note as she dropped it and is looking for it. Your friend says 'No.' What do you think you should do?

- What responsibility do you have to your friend?
- Is it right to let people lie?
- Is it right to lie for them when they have done something wrong?
- What rules could your group have about lying and how to behave when someone you know lies?
- How could your group see that they are carried out?

Scenarios

Scenario 3

In a lesson your teacher asks you to work in groups of four. Your two friends join you and another pupil is told to join the group. One of your friends begins to make nasty comments to the pupil who has joined your group. The pupil has a burn scar on his face caused by a firework burning him when he was little. Your friends laugh when they see the boy is upset. Not much work has been done. What do you think you should do?

- What can you say to your friends?
- Do they understand what verbal bullying is?
- Is it right for people to make nasty comments, which they know will upset someone?
- How do you help the person who has been bullied?
- What rules could your group develop about verbal bullying?
- How could your group see that they are carried out?

Scenario 4

A new pupil has joined the class. She is from a different country and does not speak English very well yet. Her clothes are different from the rest of the class and she eats different food from the others at lunchtime. Some of the class ignore her and others tease her. Some try to make her feel welcome and are interested in making friends with her.

- How do you think the class should treat her?
- Is it right for some to ignore her?
- Why do you think some of the class bully her by teasing her?
- Why are people treated differently if they are not the same as us?
- Is this the right way to behave?
- What rules could your group develop to ensure newcomers are treated fairly?
- How could your group see that they are carried out?

Scenarios

Scenario 5

The school playground is a mess. There is a lot of litter left after each break. The classrooms are untidy as people do not clear up after them when they have been cutting and sticking!

The Headteacher has asked the school community to be more thoughtful and to respect their environment more. Pupils do not think they should have to pick up litter or clean up after themselves.

'There are cleaners,' they say.

The cleaners have a lot more work to do because the school community is messy. The cleaners feel that the school community is not treating them with respect.

The pupils are also helping to clear a forest area near them, as it is messy. They want to make the environment better in the forest area.

- Are they right to make the forest area better?
- Are they right to think that they should not have to clean up after themselves in school?
- Do the pupils and staff in the school have a responsibility to look after the school environment?
- Is it wrong for the school community to make more work for the cleaners?
- What rules could your group develop to ensure that the environment improves in school?
- How could the group see that they are carried out?

Scenario 6

Your group has a problem. You have been asked to explain what 'right' and 'wrong' are. A new pupil has asked 'How do people know what is right and wrong?' The group has to decide what is right and what is wrong but where do they get their ideas of right and wrong from? Is there such a thing as right and wrong?

- What is right?
- What is wrong?
- How do you know?
- What is the group's answer to the question the new pupil has asked?

Challenge 7

Victorian art and music

Teacher's notes

Purposes

- To stimulate curiosity about Victorian culture.
- To research Victorian art and music and comment on the findings.
- To begin to appreciate the work of different Victorian artists and musicians.
- To develop thinking, planning and time management skills.

Aim

- To find out about the artists and musicians of Victorian times and to write a biography about one artist and one musician.
- To produce a brochure inviting people to an exhibition of the art and music of Victorian times.

Resources required

The pupil will need copies of the following:

1	'Challenge sheet'	page 143
2	'My action planning sheet'	page 144
3	'Task sheets'	pages 103 and 104
4	'Planning guidelines'	page 105
5	'Resources' sheet	page 106
6	'Record sheet'	page 107
7	'Biography guide'	page 108
8	'Discussion sheet'	page 109
9	'Brochure guide'	page 110
10	'Skills sheets'	pages 145–148

The teacher's role

1 Introducing the challenge

Write the following into the top box of a copy of the 'Challenge sheet' (page 143):

You are going to find out about the art and music of Victorian times.

You are then going to work in a small group to produce a brochure that invites people to an exhibition of the art and music of Victorian times.

Then photocopy the 'Challenge sheet' and give it to the pupils. Alternatively, they could be given a blank copy of the sheet and write the challenge on it themselves. It is important for them to have the challenge to refer to.

2 Providing support for the task sheets

Using the 'Record sheet'
This sheet provides a framework for note-taking and recording information found about the artists and musicians. Each pupil will need four copies of the sheet. The more able pupils should be able to develop their information further when they complete the 'other interesting information' section of this sheet. The rest of the class could work with the teacher in a more directed way to complete a record sheet together.

Using the 'Biography guide'
This sheet will help the pupils when writing their biography of a Victorian artist and musician. It encourages them to use the information they found out during research in a more structured way and will help them develop skills of writing information in their own words, rather than copying text from books and other sources. This piece of writing will also develop the pupils' skills of critical analysis and explanation. Discuss the sheet with them, especially the section on 'Things to think about'. Help them to decide how they want to present their subject to the reader.

Using the 'Discussion sheet'
This sheet will prove a useful guide for the pupils when carrying out the initial activities on 'Task sheet 2'. It will direct their group and paired discussions and will help them to have a more structured approach when deciding what to do. Discuss the sheet with them so that they understand the tasks and how they should work together. Remind them about the importance of listening carefully and valuing what others say.

Using the 'Brochure guide'
This guide will help the pupils plan and write their brochure. You will need to decide if they are going to put on a real exhibition or not because this will affect the content of the brochure. They will be more motivated to create an effective brochure if they have a 'real' purpose. The audience needs to be agreed first – will the visitors be other pupils in the class or school or will they be parents or members of the community?

3 Other points to note

Introduce to the pupils the concept that history can be seen through different subjects such as art and music. Encourage discussion about what they already know about the art and music during this period of time before the research begins. The resource sheet provides ideas for starting points for this research.

Questions that could be asked include:

- 'Do you know of any artists or musicians from Victorian times?'
- 'What type of music/art do you think was produced at this time?'

Show the pupils examples of Victorian art/music which can be compared with each other. Ask 'How was the work made? What sort of ideas/visual information does it give us?' For the music examples, the pupils could evaluate each piece by comparing it with the others and deciding what type of music it is. They could also decide what type of occasion the music may have been for.

Remind the pupils how to record and acknowledge the sources they have used in their research and explain how useful this is should they need to return to a source to find out more at another time.

Accepted format:
author's last name, author's initial or first name, date of publication in brackets, title of publication in italics, place of publication, publisher's name. For example:

Dowswell, Paul, (2000) *History Through Poetry - Victorians.* London: Hodder Wayland

The brochure itself should be drafted out first and different ideas tried for different effects. Guide the pupils in their choice of a suitable word processing/desktop publishing program with which to design their brochure. The contribution of local artists and musicians who have an interest in the period would enhance the pupils' understanding and would greatly benefit the planning and content of a 'real' exhibition.

You may need to act as an events organiser in order to bring the exhibition to a successful conclusion.

Links to the National Curriculum

English – Speaking and Listening

Level 4: Pupils talk and listen in an increasing range of contexts. Pupils listen carefully and make useful contributions.
Level 5: Talk engages the interest of the listener.

Ideas are developed and questions asked. Close attention is paid to what others say.

English – Reading

Level 4: Pupils locate and use ideas and information.
Level 5: Pupils show understanding of a range of texts and collate information from a range of sources.

English – Writing

Level 4: Ideas are developed in interesting ways.
Level 5: Writing conveys meaning in a range of forms for the reader.
Vocabulary choices are imaginative and appropriate.

History

Level 4: Pupils describe people from a period in history. They can select information from different sources.
Level 5: Pupils can select and evaluate sources of information and identify those useful for particular tasks.

ICT

Level 4: Pupils can use ICT to present information in different formats and show awareness of intended audience.
Level 5: Pupils can assess use of ICT in their work and make improvements.

Art

Level 4: Pupils can compare and comment on others' work.
Level 5: Pupils can analyse and comment on ideas in others' work.

Music

Level 4: Pupils can describe, compare and evaluate different types of music using an appropriate musical vocabulary.
Level 5: Pupils can evaluate how venue, time, occasion and purpose affects the way music is created.

Links to Literacy Framework

Year 5, Term 2

Word level work
W3 – use dictionaries and IT spell-checks.

Sentence level work
S3 – to adapt writing for different audiences and purposes.

Text level work
T16 – to prepare for reading by identifying what they already know and what they need to find out.
T17 – to locate information confidently and efficiently.
T18 – to know how authors record and acknowledge their sources.
T20 – to make notes.
T23 – to record and acknowledge sources in their writing.
T24 – to evaluate their work.

Assessment sheet Victorian art and music

Name: _____ Date: _____

	Achieved	To achieve
Speaking and Listening: **Level 4:** • Talks and listens in an increasing range of contexts. • Listens carefully and makes useful contributions. **Level 5:** • Talk engages the interest of the listener. • Ideas are developed, questions asked. • Pays close attention to what others say. **Reading:** **Level 4:** • Information is located and used. **Level 5:** • Shows understanding of a range of texts and collates information from a range of sources. **Writing:** **Level 4:** • Can write in a range of forms and writing is developed in interesting ways. • Spelling and punctuation is generally accurate. **Level 5:** • Meaning is conveyed in an appropriate form. **History:** **Level 4:** • Pupil describes people from a period in history. • Can select information from different sources. **Level 5:** • Can evaluate sources of information and identify those useful for particular tasks. **ICT:** **Level 4:** • Can use ICT to present information in different formats and show awareness of intended audience. **Level 5:** • Can assess use of ICT in their work and make improvements.		

Task sheet 1

Finding out about Victorian artists and musicians

Aim

To find out about the artists and musicians of Victorian times and to write a biography about one artist and one musician.

Tasks

- Use the **My action planning sheet** to help you plan your work.

- **Write** down in note form what you already know about the music or art of Victorian times. Share this with your teacher and others in your group.

- Queen Victoria was born in 1820 and died in 1901. **Find out** the names of two famous artists and two famous musicians who lived during that period. Use the **Resources sheet** to help you.

- **Write** down information about these people using a **Record sheet** for each one.

- **Find out** where the Victorians went to listen to music and to see art in your local area. Use the **Resources sheet** to help you. **Draw a map** to show where they went.

- **Choose** a piece of music or a painting you like and present it to others in your group. Explain why you like it and what it is about.

- **Write a biography** about ONE Victorian artist and ONE Victorian musician. Use the **biography guide** to help you.

  Remember to explain:

    - who they are;
    - when they lived;
    - what they did;
    - why you like their work.

Task sheet 2

Producing a brochure

Aim

To produce a brochure inviting people to an exhibition on Victorian art and music.

Tasks

• Use the **My action planning sheet** to help you plan your work.

• Using the **Discussion sheet** to guide you, carry out the following:

   − tell the people in your group about the artists and musicians you researched in Task sheet 1. Tell them what you think of their work;

   − as a group, choose which artists and musicians you would select to be part of an exhibition;

   − in pairs, decide what kind of exhibition you would like to plan and where it will be held.

• **Find out** how exhibitions are organised. **Find out** how the Victorians advertised their exhibitions. Use the **Resources sheet** to help you.

• **Plan** and **create** a brochure inviting people to attend your exhibition. Use the **brochure guide** to help you. Edit and improve your work. Decide on a suitable computer program to produce your finished brochure.

Extension work

• Imagine you are a Victorian artist or musician. Draw a picture or compose a piece of music that Victorians would like. Write a letter to a friend explaining what your work is about.

Planning guidelines

What to do

1. Read the task sheets carefully then make up your action plan of tasks to do and when to do them by completing the 'My action planning sheet'. Ask your teacher to help you with anything you are not sure of.

2. When finding out about the Victorian artists and musicians, use the 'Resources' sheet to help you.

   Use a dictionary to help you with the meaning of any words you do not understand.

3. Keep a record of the sources of information you use to find out the information – you will need this to add it to the end of your biographies.

4. Agree with your teacher who the audience for the exhibition will be – other children, parents or members of your community?

5. Collect some brochures and discuss with a partner how they are designed. Look at how the pictures, text and colour are used. Think about the way Victorians designed their posters. You may make your brochure like a Victorian one or you may make it like a modern one.

6. When planning your brochure, remember to use the 'Brochure guide'. Think carefully about the purpose of the brochure and who will be reading it.

7. Choose a suitable computer program to set out your brochure, Make sure you read it through carefully and edit it to improve it. Think carefully about the type of font to use and whether or not you will illustrate the brochure in some way.

Resources

Victorian art and music

Internet	www.victorianartinbritain.co.uk/artists.htm www.victorianartinbritain.co.uk/paintings,htm www.snaithprimary.eril.net/victoria.htm www.snaithprimary.eril.net/musintro.htm	Try CD-Rom encyclopaedias
Speakers and other sources	An events organiser could be invited to give a talk on how to organise an event and advertise it. Local musicians and artists could talk about and explain Victorian Art and Music. Microsoft Publisher has a brochures template.	Contact by writing or phoning – ask your teacher first.
Libraries	The local librarian could help you find relevant books on the subject for your research. Check your school library. Art books and music books often have the information you want. Victorian art can be found in: *Miss Carter Came With Us* by Helen Bradley. ISBN 0 224 00891 9 Reader's Digest *Life in the Victorian Age* ISBN 0 276 42121 3	The librarian will help you.
Visits	Plan a visit to your local art gallery and museum. The education officer may be able to help with your research.	These can be individual or group visits. Discuss places to visit with friends.
Audience	Your group, teacher and visitors to the exhibition.	
Your own ideas	Talk about your ideas to your group and your teacher.	Discuss your ideas with friends and your teacher.

Record sheet

name of artist/ musician	
date and place of birth	
date of death	
where the person lived	
names of works by this person	
important facts about this person's life	
other interesting information	

Victorian art and music

Features of a biography

usually written in the third person

tells the reader about the person's life and achievements

usually about someone famous

past tense

use of time connectives

Remember

Check your spelling and punctuation.

Record the sources of information you used in your research about this person.

Biography

A biography is the life-story of a person written by another author.

You are going to write a biography about ONE Victorian artist and ONE Victorian musician.

My biography

Things to think about

Decide what you want the readers to know about this person and why these things are important.

Make a list of all the important facts you want to use.

Decide if you will use pictures in your biography.

Introduction

Say who the person is.

Say when and where they were born.

Provide information about their early life.

Development

Tell the reader what the person did during their life.

Write about any important events.

Say why they were important.

Conclusion

Say why you like their work.

Give an example of their work that you like.

Say what makes you think this person's work is a good example of Victorian art or music.

Victorian art and music

Discussion sheet

Presentation to your group

1. Introduce the artist or musician you are going to talk about.
2. Say when and where they were born and died. Present some interesting facts about them.
3. Show examples of their work if you are able to.
4. Say which artist and musician you prefer and explain why you like their work.
5. Ask the group for their comments. Listen carefully to them and reply if you need to.

Group discussion

1. Choose a chairperson. His/her role is to see that the discussion is polite and everyone gets a chance to speak and is listened to.
2. Individuals can suggest a person and explain why they would include them in the exhibition.
3. After all the musicians and artists have been discussed fully, the group should decide who they will include in their exhibition.
4. The chairperson should check with the teacher to see how many people can be included in the exhibition.
5. The chairperson can ask the group to vote on each person and ask a recorder to write down the person's name and how many votes they get.
6. The chairperson announces the number of votes and who is in the exhibition.

Paired discussion

WILL WE HAVE THE COMPOSER'S MUSIC PLAYING?

1. Use your research about how exhibitions are organised to help you to plan your exhibition.
2. Think about the people you are including in your exhibition. What can you write about them that is interesting?
3. What order would you want people to see the exhibits in?
4. Would you have Victorian composers' music playing?
5. Design a layout for the exhibition. Draw a plan of it. Think about the place in the school you are planning to put the exhibition. How much room is there? Can people get in and out easily?
6. Present your ideas to the teacher who will decide with the group which exhibition plan to use.

Remember

Check your spelling and punctuation.

Make sure you have included all the important information such as date, time and place of the exhibition.

If you are using a computer program to do your brochure, remember to save it as you go.

Edit your work to make improvements.

Drafting

Decide which computer program you will use to set out your brochure.

Remember to save it as you go.

Discuss your draft with your teacher – does it include everything? Is it eye-catching?

Does the exhibition sound exciting?

Edit your draft before printing a final version.

My brochure

Things to think about

Who is the brochure for? Who will read it?

What do you want the readers to think when they look at your brochure?

How do you want the readers to respond to it?

What style of brochure? Three page fold? Two page fold? What size will it be?

What illustrations will you use?

What size and style of font will you use?

What colours do you think will attract people's attention?

Brochure

A brochure is a pamphlet or leaflet that provides the reader with information about something.

You are going to write a brochure inviting people to an exhibition about Victorian art and music.

Features of a brochure

bold headings and sub-headings

bright colours

clearly set out text

use of illustrations to make it look interesting

all important information included

Planning

Design your brochure on paper first.

Decide where you will place different information.

Think about how to use persuasive words to encourage people to visit your exhibition.

Collect the illustrations you will use – decide where they will go.

Share your ideas with your teacher.

Victorian art and music

Electrical inventions

Teacher's notes

Purposes

- To find out how electricity was discovered and developed.

- To consider how electrical inventions have made our lives easier and more comfortable.

- To develop reasoning and analytical skills.

- To write an explanation text.

- To develop skills of persuasive presentations.

- To develop thinking, planning and time management skills.

Aims

- To find out about Michael Faraday who invented the electric motor and write a biography about him.

- To write an explanation of how an electrical invention works and to present and explain a display which shows how this invention has made our lives better.

Resources required

The pupil will need copies of the following:

1	'Challenge sheet'	page 143
2	'My action planning sheet'	page 144
3	'Task sheets'	pages 114 and 115
4	'Planning guidelines'	page 116
5	'Resources' sheet	page 117
6	'Biography guide'	page 118
7	'Explanation writing guide'	page 119
8	'Presentation guide'	page 120
9	'Skills sheets'	page 145–148

The teacher's role

1 Introducing the challenge

Write the following into the top box of a copy of the 'Challenge sheet' (page 143):

You are going to write a biography about Michael Faraday who invented the electric motor.

You are then going to choose an electrical invention, write an explanation of how it works and prepare, present and explain a display about this invention and how it has made our lives better.

Then photocopy the 'Challenge sheet' and give it to the pupils. Alternatively, they could be given a blank copy of the sheet and write the challenge on it themselves. It is important for them to have the challenge to refer to.

2 Providing support for the task sheets

Using the 'Biography guide'
This sheet will help the pupils when writing their biography of Michael Faraday. It encourages them to use the information they found during research in a more structured way and will help them develop skills of writing information in their own words, rather than copying text from books and other sources. This piece of writing will also develop their skills of critical analysis and explanation.

Using the 'Explanation writing guide'
This sheet will prove a very useful guide for the pupils when writing their explanation of how their chosen electrical invention works. It is important that they understand the type of writing they are expected to do and are guided through the writing process. Encourage them to share their writing with others to ensure that the reader is able to follow the explanation clearly and logically and that a concise explanation of how the invention works is achieved. The use of labelled diagrams will be very important when explaining their chosen invention.

Using the 'Presentation guide'
This guide will help the pupils plan and present their display and presentation to the class. The presentations could be carried out after a whole class topic on electrical circuits in order to show how science has a real role to play in our lives.

3 Other points to note

Before commencing the activities on 'Task sheet 1', discuss with the pupils what they already know about the discovery and development of electricity. Have they heard of Michael Faraday before? What do they already know about him? Do they know who Andre Ampere, Benjamin Franklin, George Ohm, Alessandro Volta and Luigi Galvani were, for example? Do they know what these scientists discovered?

Guide the pupils in finding the answers to the questions asked on 'Task sheet 1'. The whole class could write the biography of Michael Faraday together with the teacher modelling the writing, but the more able should be able to write independently in greater depth about each of the specific areas mentioned on the task sheet.

Remind the pupils how to record and acknowledge the sources they have used in their research and explain how useful this is should they need to return to a source to find out more at another time.

Accepted format
author's last name, author's initial or first name, date of publication in brackets, title of publication in italics, place of publication, publisher's name. For example:

Walpole, Brenda, (1991) *Junior Illustrated Encyclopaedia – Science*. London: Kingfisher Books

Expand the questions on 'Task sheet 2' and make a separate discussion sheet for the pupils to complete with spaces for 'Note your initial ideas about why the invention makes our lives better', 'Has the invention changed the way we live in any way?', 'Has it changed how we shop, travel to work and use our leisure time?' and 'Make notes about who invented the invention you chose.'

It would also be useful to have a whole class discussion about the effectiveness of displays – perhaps beginning with those in the classroom and extending to those in other parts of the school and the local community. What makes a display effective? How can they attract people's attention? What is their purpose? What features do you think a good display has? What features does a poor display have?

Guide the pupils in their choice of electrical invention to ensure they are able to find out enough information about how it works and how it impacts on our lives.

The teacher will need to help the pupils decide how best to present their talk and how long it should be. The audience will probably be the pupils' own class but the presentations could be given to other classes or to parents. The teacher should discuss with the pupils how knowing what audience the presentation is aimed at will impact on the way the talk is given and its content.

Finally, the teacher needs to share ideas with the pupils about how they can make their presentation persuasive in order to convince the listeners that their chosen invention truly has made our lives easier. What type of persuasive words and phrases will they use? Can they demonstrate a point they want to make in a concrete way?

Links to the National Curriculum

English – Speaking and Listening

Level 4: Pupils' talk is adapted to the purpose. Ideas are developed and contributions made.
Level 5: Pupils vary their expression and vocabulary. In discussion, they pay close attention to what others say, ask questions to develop ideas.

English – Reading

Level 4: Pupils refer to texts when explaining their views.
Level 5: Pupils show understanding of a range of texts. They retrieve and collate information from a range of sources.

English – Writing

Level 4: Pupils' ideas are developed and sustained in interesting ways for the reader.
Level 5: Writing conveys meaning in a range of forms. Vocabulary choices are imaginative and used precisely.

Science

Level 4: Pupils select information from sources provided.
Level 5: Pupils select from a range of sources of information.

History

Level 4: Pupils are beginning to select and combine information from different sources.
Level 5: Pupils select and organise information to produce structured work, making appropriate use of dates and terms.

Links to Literacy Framework

Year 5, Term 2

Word level work
W3 – use dictionaries and IT spell-checks.

Sentence level work
S3 – to adapt writing for different audiences and purposes.
S5 – to use punctuation effectively.

Text level work
T16 – to prepare for reading by identifying what they already know and what they need to find out.
T17 – to locate information confidently and efficiently.
T18 – to know how authors record and acknowledge their sources.
T20 – to make notes.
T21 – to convert notes into writing for others to read.
T22 – to plan, edit and refine explanatory texts.
T23 – to record and acknowledge sources in their writing.
T24 – to evaluate their work.

Assessment sheet

Name: ———————————————— **Date:** ————————————

	Achieved	To achieve

Speaking and Listening:

Level 4:
- Talk is adapted to the purpose.
- Ideas are developed and contributions made.

Level 5:
- Talk engages the interest of the listener.
- Expression and vocabulary is varied.
- Pays close attention in discussion – develops ideas.

Reading:

Level 4:
- Information is located and used.
- Refers to text when explaining views.

Level 5:
- Shows understanding of a range of texts and collates information from a range of sources.

Writing:

Level 4:
- Can write in a range of forms and writing is developed in interesting ways.
- Spelling and punctuation is generally accurate.

Level 5:
- Meaning is conveyed in an appropriate form.
- Vocabulary is used precisely.

History:

Level 4:
- Can select information from different sources.

Level 5:
- Can select and combine information to produce structured work, making appropriate use of dates and terms.

Science:

Level 4:
- Can select information from sources provided.

Level 5:
- Can select from a range of sources of information.

Task sheet 1

Finding out about Michael Faraday

Aim

To find out about Michael Faraday who invented the electric motor and write a biography about him.

Michael Faraday

Tasks

- Use the **My action planning sheet** to help you plan your work.

- **Find out** about the life of Michael Faraday who was a blacksmith's son. Find out about his life as a child. How did working as a bookbinder's apprentice help him to become a scientist? Write down what you find out in note form. Use the **Resources sheet** to help you.

- **Find out** why Michael Faraday introduced the Faraday lectures in 1827. Add this to your notes.

- In 1831, Michael Faraday invented the electrical transformer. **Find out** what this was. **Draw** a diagram of it. **Write** an explanation of why it was such an important discovery. Add this information to your notes.

- Using your notes, **write** a biography of the important events in Faraday's life. Use the **Biography guide** to help you. Remember to explain:
  - who he was;
  - when he lived;
  - what he did;
  - why his work was so important.

Task sheet 2

Giving a presentation

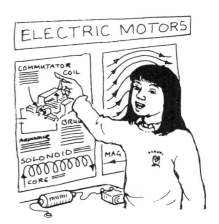

Aim

To present and explain how an electrical invention has changed our lives for the better.

Tasks

- Use the **My action planning sheet** to help you plan your work.

- In pairs, do the following:

  - **find out** about different electrical inventions (old or new) you are interested in;

  - **choose** one of these inventions and make notes about:

    who invented it and when;

    why you think this invention makes our lives better;

    whether or not this invention has changed the way we live;

  Use the **Resources sheet** to help you.

- **Write** a short explanation about how your chosen invention works. Use the **explanation writing guide** to help you.

- **Plan** and **prepare** a **display** about this invention. Plan and practise a presentation about your display that will convince others that your invention has improved our lives. Use the **presentation guide** to help you.

Extension work

- Choose a science fiction film. Write about the scientific inventions in it. Compare these with what we have now and what we might have in the future.

Planning guidelines

What to do

1. Read the task sheets carefully then make up your action plan of tasks to do and when to do them by completing the 'My action planning sheet'. Ask your teacher to help you with anything you are not sure of.

2. When finding out about Michael Faraday, use the resources sheet to help you. Use more than one source of information to find out as much as you can about him. Remember to ask your teacher's permission before you contact anyone or use the internet.

   Use a dictionary to help you with the meaning of any words you do not understand.

3. Keep a record of the sources of information you use to find out the information – you will need this to add it to the end of your biography. Use the biography guide to help you write your biography.

4. Choose your electrical invention with care – can you find out enough information about it, how it works and who invented it? Remember – you must be able to convince others how this invention has drastically improved our lives.

5. When writing your explanation, use the explanation writing guide to help you. Remember to use labelled diagrams because these will help others understand your explanation better.

6. Agree with your teacher who the audience for your presentation will be – this may affect the type of display and talk you give. You will also need to agree the type of display you can put up in your classroom and where it will be.

   If you have access to a multimedia presentation program such as Powerpoint, your teacher may allow you to use this. Make sure you know how it works.

7. Make sure you practise your presentation. Is there a set time limit? How will you convince others that your chosen invention has improved their lives?

Resources

Internet	www.rigb.org/heritage/faradaypage.html http://scienceworld.wolfram.com/biography/Faraday.html www.bbc.co.uk/history/historic_figures/faraday_michael.shtml www.schoolscience.co.uk/flash/electric/index.htm	Try CD-Rom encyclopaedias
Speakers and other sources	Speakers from the energy industry – the local electricity board may have education officers and material that is helpful. Someone from an electrical goods retail outlet will be able to give information about modern uses of electrical inventions and technologies.	Contact by writing or phoning – ask your teacher first.
Libraries	The reference and fiction sections of the library will have books that will help you with your research.	The librarian will help you.
Visits	The local Museum may have an exhibition or artefacts showing the use of electric inventions. A visit to a local factory that makes appliances. A visit to a retail outlet to see what people buy.	These can be individual or group visits. Discuss places to visit with friends.
Audience	Your group, friends, teacher and visitors.	
Your own ideas	Discuss your ideas with your teacher, friends and research partner.	Discuss your ideas with friends and your teacher.

Features of a biography

usually written in the third person

tells the reader about the person's life and achievements

usually about someone famous

past tense

use of time connectives

Biography

A biography is the life-story of a person written by another author.

You are going to write a biography about Michael Faraday.

Remember

Check your spelling and punctuation.

Record the sources of information you used in your research about this person.

Michael Faraday

Introduction

Say who Faraday was.

Say when and where he was born.

Provide information about his childhood.

Things to think about

Decide what you want the readers to know about this person and why these things are important.

Make a list of all the important facts you want to use.

Decide if you will use pictures in your biography.

Development

Tell the reader what Faraday did during his life.

Write about any important events, such as becoming a bookbinder's apprentice.

Say why these events were important.

Conclusion

Say why Faraday's work was important and how it has helped ordinary people's lives to be better.

Electrical inventions

Features of an explanation

has a title that asks a question or says what the explanation is going to be about

begins with a general statement to introduce the topic

contains a series of logical steps to explain the process/thing

present tense

impersonal style

uses technical words

uses logical connectives such as 'because' and 'so'

often has complex sentences

often uses diagrams

My explanation

An explanation

An explanation explains how or why something happens.

You are going to write an explanation of how your chosen electrical invention works.

Things to think about

Plan the steps of your explanation carefully – will the reader be able to understand what you mean?

Decide which diagrams to use – make sure they are very simple and clearly labelled.

Introduction

Briefly say what it is that you are going to explain.

Development

Tell the reader, in logical sequence, how the invention works.

Use labelled diagrams to support this explanation.

Conclusion

Briefly sum up what you have explained.

Say why this invention is so important.

Remember

Make sure you have included all the necessary information.

Practise presenting your display before you do the presentation.

Try to make your talk interesting so your audience will want to listen!

Use of ICT

Think about how you can use ICT to enhance your presentation - such as word processing or Powerpoint.

My presentation

A presentation

A presentation is an illustrated talk presenting information to an audience.

You are going to plan and give a presentation about an electrical invention explaining how the invention has made people's lives better. You are going to use a display to illustrate your talk.

Things to think about

What do you want the display to look like?
What pictures and poster will you use?
How will you make headings stand out?
What style and size of font will you use?
Will you word process your labels/captions or write them?
How will you attract people's attention to your display?
What information will you use?
How long will your talk be?
How will you convince the audience that this invention has improved people's lives?

Planning

Draw out the design of your display on paper first.

Write out the information you will use.

Think about how to use persuasive words.

Decide what pictures you will use in your display.

Think about who the display and talk are for - are they appropriate for them?

Adventure playgrounds

Teacher's notes

Purposes

- To consider the uses of the school playground and open spaces.

- To investigate the opportunities that pupils have to undertake activities within the school grounds to develop strength, agility and coordination skills.

- To develop observation, investigation and analytical skills.

- To write logically and persuasively.

- To develop skills of making presentations.

- To develop thinking, planning and time management skills.

Aim

- To investigate the opportunities for keeping fit in the playground and other open spaces in our school.

- To design and make a model of an adventure playground for school and to give a presentation to others about your ideas.

Resources required

The pupil will need copies of the following:

1	'Challenge sheet'	page 143
2	'My action planning sheet'	page 144
3	'Task sheets'	pages 125 and 126
4	'Planning guidelines'	page 127
5	'Resources' sheet	page 128
5	'Observation sheet'	page 129
6	'Formal letter guide'	page 130
7	'Presentation guide'	page 131
9	'Skills sheets'	pages 145–148

The teacher's role

1 Introducing the challenge

Write the following into the top box of a copy of the 'Challenge sheet' (page 143):

> You are going to investigate the opportunities for keeping fit in your school playground and other open spaces.

You are then going to design and make a model of an adventure playground for your school and give a presentation to others about your ideas.

Then photocopy the 'Challenge sheet' and give it to the pupils. Alternatively, they could be given a blank copy of the sheet and write the challenge on it themselves. It is important for them to have the challenge to refer to.

2 Providing support for the task sheets

Using the 'Observation sheet'

Before using this sheet, discuss with the pupils how they might go about carrying out the observations. Should we inform the other pupils and staff that we are conducting a survey (perhaps at assembly time)? Are there any safety considerations?

Also discuss the definitions of the terms 'strength', 'agility' and 'coordination'. How will the pupils be able to categorise the activities they observe correctly? Will some activities fit all three categories? The pupils may need to break down the activities they observe into smaller skills; for example, playing football can be broken down into passing the ball, shooting goals, running, stopping the ball, heading the ball, dodging opponents and so on. Such close observation will finely tune the pupils' observation skills.

Examples of activities for each category include:
- Strength – hanging from and moving along bars, sit ups, press ups, swimming distances;

- Agility – skipping, dribbling balls, gymnastics;

- Coordination – shooting goals, hitting a ball with a racquet/bat, passing a ball, following a sequence of moves in a dance, gymnastics.

Once the pupils are ready to carry out their observations, go through the sheet with them to make sure they understand what to do. It may be beneficial for them to work in pairs to take turns in observing and recording.

Using the 'Formal letter guide'

This sheet will be a very useful guide for the pupils when writing their letter to the headteacher requesting the building of an adventure playground at school. (If your school already has excellent playground facilities, this challenge could be aimed at a local park, for example.) Writing the letter will develop the pupils' persuasive writing skills!

Challenge 9 continued — Adventure playgrounds

Using the 'Presentation guide'
This guide will help the pupils to plan and prepare their presentation. They will need to research playground equipment and safety issues as well as plan and make their model playgrounds. Teacher guidance is important at this stage to ensure they understand health and safety issues.

3 Other points to note

The pupils may need guidance when they come to draw their plan of the playground. They need to understand that the plan should be drawn as if from a bird's eye view and they may want to use a key of some sort to indicate different aspects.

As part of 'Task sheet 1' the pupils are asked to consider the other open spaces in the school grounds. Guide their discussions and help them understand the importance of using the school grounds to their best advantage. Make them aware of how 'playing' can actually be helping to build fitness and strength and is therefore a very important part of the school day.

Also, remind them about accessibility in their playground – can people in wheelchairs have access, for example?

Remind them about the format for a formal letter and the type of language that is used. Model an example letter as a guide, showing how persuasive language can be used together with the information that needs to be provided. Forewarn the headteacher who will hopefully be able to make a written response to the letters thereby giving the task a real purpose. A school governor might also be a helpful recipient of the pupils' letters.

Help them to decide how they can make notes as they are researching equipment. They may need reminding of the following:

- information can be abbreviated and listed as bullet points;
- key words can be underlined;
- sticky-notes can be useful for marking information pages in books;
- information can be recorded in a chart or table;
- diagrams and drawings make useful summaries of information.

It would be beneficial to have a whole class discussion about model making. What resources are available to use? What kinds of materials would be most suitable? What equipment will be used? What safety considerations need to be taken into account when making the model? How large will the model be? What is its purpose? Where will it be displayed? How will it be labelled? Are models more effective than plans?

Help the pupils to decide how best to present their talk and how long it should be. Decide who the audience will be – the headteacher, the governors, other pupils, a builder? Discuss with the pupils how knowing what audience the presentation is aimed at will impact on the way the talk is given and its content.

Finally, share ideas with the pupils about how they can make their presentation persuasive in order to convince the listeners that their playground design is not only well thought out and safe but also essential to the fitness of the pupils at the school. What type of persuasive words and phrases will they use? Can they demonstrate a point they want to make in a concrete way?

NOTE: Useful websites
http://tlfe.org.uk/scienceks1and2.htm

www.bbc.co.uk/schools/revisewise/science/physical/11_act.shtml

www.primaryresources.co.uk/science/science/4.htm

Links to the National Curriculum
English – Speaking and Listening
Level 4: Pupils develop ideas thoughtfully and convey opinions clearly.
Level 5: Pupils use standard English in formal situations.
Pupils talk confidently in a range of contexts

English – Reading
Level 4: Pupils locate and use information through detailed reading.
Level 5: Pupils identify and select relevant information to support their views.

English – Writing
Level 4: Pupils' writing is organised appropriately for the purpose of the reader.
Level 5: Pupils' writing is interesting and conveys meaning clearly in appropriate forms.
Words with complex regular patterns are spelt correctly.

Design and Technology
Level 4: Pupils generate ideas by collecting information.
They communicate ideas using words, sketches and models.
Can take user's views into account.
Level 5: Pupils clarify ideas through discussion, drawing and modelling.
Pupils can reflect on their design as it develops and identify what could be improved.

_act

122 Literacy *for the more able*

Challenge 9 continued

Physical Education

Level 4: Pupils apply basic safety principles in preparing for exercise.
Can explain how exercise affects the body.
Level 5: Pupils understand why physical activity is good for health and well-being.

Links to Literacy Framework

Year 5, Term 3

Word level work
W3 – use dictionaries and IT spell-checks.

Sentence level work
S2 – to understand how writing can be adapted for different audiences and purposes.
S4 – to use punctuation marks accurately in complex sentences.
S7 – to use connectives.

Text level work
T16 – to make notes.
T17 – to draft and write letters for real purposes.

Assessment sheet

Adventure playgrounds

Name: _____ Date: _____

	Achieved	To achieve
Speaking and Listening:		
Level 4:		
• Can develop ideas thoughtfully and convey opinions clearly.		
Level 5:		
• Can use standard English in formal situations.		
• Can talk confidently in a range of contexts		
Reading:		
Level 4:		
• Can locate and use information through detailed reading.		
Level 5:		
• Can identify and select relevant information to support his/her views.		
Writing:		
Level 4:		
• Writing is organised appropriately for the purpose of the reader.		
Level 5:		
• Writing is interesting and conveys meaning clearly in appropriate forms.		
• Words with complex regular patterns are spelt correctly.		
Design & Technology:		
Level 4:		
• Can generate ideas by collecting information.		
• Can take user's views into account.		
• Can communicate ideas using words, sketches and models.		
Level 5:		
• Can clarify ideas through discussion, drawing and modelling.		
• Can reflect on their design as it develops and identify what could be improved.		
Physical education:		
Level 4:		
• Can apply basic safety principles in preparing for exercise.		
• Can explain how exercise affects the body.		
Level 5:		
• Understands why physical activity is good for health and well-being.		

Task sheet 1

Finding out about our school grounds

Aim

To investigate the opportunities for keeping fit in the playground and other open spaces in our school.

Tasks

- Use the **My action planning sheet** to help you plan your work.

- At break or lunch time **observe** the type of activities that children do in the playground. **Record** the following things on the **observation sheet**:

  - the types of activities that develop strength, agility and coordination;

  - other activities carried out;

  - the activities that need open spaces;

  - the activities that take place in one area only.

- **Draw a plan** of the playground that shows where different activities take place.

- At another time, **observe** how other **open spaces** (such as grassy areas, school field) in the school are used. With a partner, **discuss** the following things:

  - how you think these open spaces could be used to develop children's strength, agility and coordination skills;

  - what sort of activities and outdoor equipment could help children develop their fitness skills;

  - whether an adventure playground would help. Explain why.

  - is there access for all children, such as those who use a wheelchair?

  Make notes of your ideas.

- **Draw a plan** of the open spaces the school has that you think could be used for fitness activities.

- **Write a letter** to your headteacher asking for an adventure playground to be built in order to improve the fitness of the children in the school. Use the **Formal letter guide** to help you.

Task sheet 2

Adventure playgrounds

Giving a presentation

Aim

To make a model of an adventure playground and give a presentation to others about your ideas.

Tasks

• Use the **My action planning sheet** to help you plan your work.

• With a partner, **find out** about the type of equipment found in adventure playgrounds. **Make notes and drawings** about the things you think would be suitable for a school playground. Use the **Resources sheet** to help you.

• With your partner, **find out** how to design an adventure playground and the safety issues that need to be considered. **Make notes**.

• Using your notes and your observation sheet, **write** a short description of the items you would include in an adventure playground for your school. Say why you would include them and how they would help the fitness of those who use them. **Share your ideas** with others in your group. **Listen** to their views. **Decide** which equipment you will finally have in your design.

• **Plan and design** your adventure playground. Edit any ideas after further discussion with others in your group.

• **Make a model** of the playground and plan a talk to persuade others how your playground design would improve the fitness of the children in the school. Use the **Presentation guide** to help you.

Extension work

• Find out how much your adventure playground would cost the school to buy. Use catalogues to help you. Use a spreadsheet to show the cost of each piece of equipment.

• Contact a builder to find out how much it would cost to build.

Planning guidelines

What to do:

1. Read the task sheets carefully then make up your action plan of tasks to do and when to do them by completing the 'My action planning sheet'. Ask your teacher to help you with anything you are not sure of.

2. When making your playground observations, make sure to observe carefully and record accurately – this will have an impact on the playground design that you eventually create.

3. In your discussions, remember to think about safety issues as well as fitness ones. Only a safe playground will be accepted.

4. When doing your plans, remember to draw them as if from a bird's eye view. You may want to use a key in your plan. Ask your teacher to help you if you are unsure of what to do.

5. When writing to your headteacher use the 'Formal letter guide' to help you. Remember that you need to persuade him/her that the adventure playground is needed for health reasons.

6. Use the 'Resources' sheet to help you with your research for 'Task sheet 2'. Your information gathering is a very important part of the work. If you show that your ideas are well-researched, you have a greater chance of them being accepted.

7. Think very carefully about the design of your playground. Does it include equipment that will develop strength, agility and coordination? Have safety issues been considered? Will your design suit the setting of your school? Have all children access to the playground?

8. When making your model think carefully about the materials you will use. Remember to use equipment safely.

9. Agree with your teacher who the audience for your presentation will be – this may affect the type of talk you give.

10. Make sure you practise your presentation. Is there a set time limit? How will you convince your audience that your playground design will improve the fitness of children in your school?

Resources

Internet	www.livingwillow.fsnet.co.uk www.playgrounds.co.nz/play.htm www.thelighthouseforeducation.co.uk/fit	Try CD-Rom encyclopaedias
Speakers and other sources	Speakers from the energy industry – the local electricity board may have education officers and material that is helpful. Speaker from an electrical goods retail outlet will be able to give information about modern uses of electrical inventions and technologies.	Contact by writing or phoning – ask your teacher first.
Libraries	The reference and fiction sections of the library will have books that will help you with your research.	The librarian will help you.
Visits	The local Museum may have an exhibition or artefacts showing the use of electric inventions. A visit to a local factory that makes appliances. A visit to a retail outlet to see what people buy.	These can be individual or group visits. Discuss places to visit with friends.
Audience	Your group, friends, teacher and visitors.	
Your own ideas	Discuss your ideas with your teacher, friends and research partner.	Discuss your ideas with friends and your teacher.

Observation sheet

	strength activities	agility activities	coordination activities
List here the fitness activities you observe and enter them in the right box.	for example, hanging from bars	for example, skipping	for example, shooting goals
List here any other activities you observe.	for example, talking, reading		
List here the activities that need an open space.			
List here the activities that can take place in one area only.			

Formal letter guide
Adventure playgrounds

Features of a formal letter

writer's address in top right-hand corner with date beneath

address of recipient on left-hand side of next line

Dear (Sir, Madam or their name if known) underneath this

paragraphs to state the reason for writing and the action you want taken

formal ending ('Yours faithfully' if the recipient's name is not known, otherwise 'Yours sincerely')

usually written in the present tense

uses connectives to join sentences and paragraphs

Your headteacher's name
Your school address

Your name and address

date

Dear (headteacher's name)

I am writing to ask your permission to build an adventure playground at our school. I have researched the subject very carefully and I would like you to consider the following points:

Yours sincerely,

your signature
your name

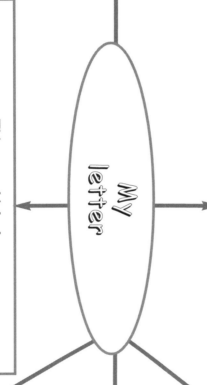

My letter

Formal letter

A formal letter can be written to inform, to complain or to persuade the reader.

You are going to write a letter to your headteacher to persuade him/her that the building of an adventure playground would greatly improve the fitness of the pupils in the school.

Introduction

How will you begin your letter?

Try to explain the purpose of your letter clearly and briefly.

Development

How will you convince the headteacher that an adventure playground is a good idea?

Use persuasive words, backed up by evidence from your observations about how the playground can improve the fitness of pupils in the school.

Conclusion

Make sure you have a good ending.

Sum up your ideas and end your letter properly.

Things to think about

Make a list of all the points you want to include in your letter - think about which order to present them.

How will you persuade the headteacher to agree with you?

Show that you have considered safety as well as fitness. Will you word process your letter?

Make sure you check it through to see if it makes sense and that the spelling and punctuation are correct.

Adventure playgrounds

My presentation

A presentation

A presentation is an illustrated talk presenting information to an audience.

You are going to plan and give a presentation that will convince your audience that building an adventure playground will improve the fitness of pupils in your school.

Remember

Make sure you have included all the necessary information.

Practise presenting your talk.

Try to make your talk interesting so your audience will want to listen!

Use of ICT

Think about how you can use ICT to enhance your presentation - such as word processing or Powerpoint.

Things to think about

How will you begin your presentation?
What information do you need to provide about what an adventure playground is?
How will you use your plan and model to explain your ideas for the playground?
How will you include research about fitness and safety issues?
How will you convince the audience that your plan is safe?
How will you use your voice?
In which order will you present your ideas?
How will you make the talk interesting?

Planning

Make sure your plan and model are well presented and include everything the audience needs to see.

Write out the information you will use in your talk.

Decide how you will persuade others that your ideas are good ones.

Challenge 10

Teeth and toothpaste

Teacher's notes

Purposes

- To find out about the functions and proper care of teeth.
- To investigate what toothpaste is made from and how using toothpaste helps to keep teeth healthy.
- To explore the purposes and effects of advertising.
- To develop skills of writing persuasively.
- To develop skills of making presentations.
- To develop thinking, planning and time management skills.

Aims

- To find out about the functions of teeth and toothpaste and to give a presentation to seven-year-olds about how to keep teeth healthy.
- To design and produce a toothpaste advertisement that will appeal to seven-year-olds.

Resources required

The pupil will need copies of the following:

1	'Challenge sheet'	page 143
2	'My action planning sheet'	page 144
3	'Task sheets'	pages 135 and 136
4	'Planning guidelines'	page 137
5	'Resources' sheet	page 138
6	'Presentation guide'	page 139
7	'Information sheet'	page 140
8	'Advertisement guide'	page 141
9	'Commentary guide'	page 142
10	'Skills sheets'	pages 145–148

The teacher's role

1 Introducing the challenge

Write the following into the top box of a copy of the 'Challenge' sheet (page 143):

You are going to find out about the functions and proper care of teeth as well as finding out what toothpaste contains and how its use helps to keep teeth healthy.

You are then going to design and produce a toothpaste advertisement that will appeal to seven-year-olds.'

Then photocopy the 'Challenge sheet' and give it to the pupils. Alternatively, they could be given a blank copy of the sheet and write the challenge on it themselves. It is important for them to have the challenge to refer to.

2 Providing support for the task sheets

Using the 'Presentation guide'
This guide will help the pupils to plan and prepare their presentation. You could arrange for each of them to give their talk to a small group of seven-year-olds from another class in the school. In this way, they will have a real purpose and audience.

Using the 'Discussion sheet'
This sheet will enable the pupils to carry out their discussions about the toothpaste advertisements in a more focused way. You will need to remind them of the differences between fact and opinion. You will also need to introduce the concept that advertisements are aimed at different target audiences – this is something that they may not have been consciously aware of before.

Help the discussions by contributing other relevant questions. For example:
- 'What part of this advert immediately has an impact on you? Why?'
- 'Who do you think this advertisement is targeted at? Why?'
- 'How noticeable is the brand name?'
- 'Look at your list of persuasive words – explain why you think they will persuade people to buy and use the toothpaste advertised.'
- 'Which toothpaste advertisements on television do you remember the most? Why do you think that is?'

Using the 'Advertisement guide'
This guide will help the pupils to plan and prepare their advertisement. Help them to target their advertisement initially at seven-year-olds. They could carry out a survey of seven-year-olds in their school before commencing their planning. They could show the children a selection of advertisements and ask them to say which ones they prefer and why – this may help them to decide which design features they will include in their own design.

Using the 'My point of view' guide

This guide will be an invaluable help to the pupils when they write their point of view about their completed advertisement. Explain that the purpose of the writing is to help other people understand their advertisement more fully. It will explain why they have used particular techniques and words in order to create specific effects. The points of view could be displayed with the advertisements to provide detailed information about them.

3   Other points to note

Before preparing the talk, guide the pupils in their research about the functions and care of teeth. The topic could be introduced as a whole class activity with the more able focusing on more extensive research.

Ask the pupils to bring in a collection of different toothpaste containers (such as tubes and pumps) as well as the outside packaging in order for the pupils to find out about the ingredients used in making the toothpastes. As part of 'Task sheet 1' the more able are required to find out about some of these ingredients in more detail. Inviting a dentist to visit would be a very worthwhile experience for this challenge.

The pupils should invent a name for their toothpaste and decide if they are going to incorporate that name into a jingle or rhyme as part of their advertisement. They will need to consider carefully the layout and how this impacts on the readers' responses. If a desktop publishing program is made available, the pupils will be able to experiment with different font styles, colours and sizes as well as background colours quickly and easily.

The teacher needs to remind the pupils that adverts have words in them that can put special images/ideas into the reader's mind. What sort of words make toothpaste interesting?

Links to the National Curriculum

English – Speaking and Listening

Level 4: Pupils convey opinions clearly.
Talk is adapted to the purpose.
Level 5: Pupils pay close attention to what others say.
Can engage the interest of the listener.
Can talk confidently in a range of contexts.

English – Reading

Level 4: Pupils can locate and use information through detailed reading.
Level 5: Pupils can identify and select relevant information.

English – Writing

Level 4: Pupils' ideas are developed in interesting ways.
Words are identified and used for effect.
Level 5: Pupils' writing is interesting and conveys meaning clearly.
Vocabulary choices are imaginative and words are used precisely.

Science

Level 4: Pupils demonstrate knowledge and understanding of life processes.
Level 5: Can describe the main functions of organs of the human body.

Design & Technology

Level 4: Pupils can generate ideas by collecting and using information.
Can reflect on their design as it develops.
Can identify what is working well and what can be improved.
Level 5: Pupils can draw on and use various sources of information.
Can evaluate their product and their use of information sources.

Links to Literacy Framework
Year 5, Term 3

Word level work

W3 – use dictionaries and IT spell-checks.

Sentence level work

S2 – to understand how writing can be adapted for different audiences and purposes.

Text level work

T14 – to read examples of adverts. To compare writing which informs and persuades.
T15 – to investigate the use of persuasive devices.
T16 – to make notes.
T18 – to write a commentary.

Assessment sheet

Name:_____ Date: _____

	Achieved	To achieve

Speaking and Listening:

Level 4:
- Can convey opinions clearly.
- Talk is adapted to the purpose.

Level 5:
- Pays close attention to what others say.
- Can engage the interest of the listener.
- Can talk confidently in a range of contexts.

Reading:

Level 4:
- Can locate and use information through detailed reading.

Level 5:
- Can identify and select relevant information.

Writing:

Level 4:
- Ideas are developed in interesting ways.
- Words are identified and used for effect.

Level 5:
- Writing is interesting and conveys meaning clearly.
- Vocabulary choices are imaginative and words are used precisely.

Science:

Level 4:
- Demonstrates knowledge and understanding of life processes.

Level 5:
- Can describe the main functions of organs of the human body.

Design & Technology:

Level 4:
- Can generate ideas by collecting and using information.
- Can reflect on his/her design as it develops.
- Can identify what is working well and what can be improved.

Level 5:
- Can draw on and use various sources of information.
- Can evaluate his/her product and their use of information sources.

Task sheet 1

Finding out about teeth and toothpaste

Aim

To find out about the functions of teeth and toothpaste and to give a presentation to seven-year-olds about how to keep teeth healthy.

Tasks

- Use the **My action planning sheet** to help you plan your work.

- In a group, discuss all the different types and brands of toothpaste that you know about. **Make a list** of them.

- Using a collection of toothpaste containers and packaging, **make notes** about the following:

  – the ingredients contained in the toothpaste;

  – the information given that tells you what toothpaste is for and how to use it.

- Now **find out** the meaning of the following words:

  plaque, decay, sodium fluoride, hydrated silica, sorbitol, xanthan gum, titanium dioxide, sodium saccharin

  Use the **Resources sheet** and **dictionaries** to help you.

- **Find out** all you can about teeth - what they are used for and how to care for them properly. **Make notes** about this information. Use the **Resources sheet** to help you.

- Imagine you are a dentist. Use your notes to **plan and prepare a talk** to a group of seven-year-olds about what their teeth are for and how using toothpaste will keep their teeth healthy. Use the **Presentation guide** to help you. Perhaps you can dress as a dentist when you give your talk!

Task sheet 2

Designing an advertisement

Aim

To design an advertisement for a new toothpaste that will appeal to seven-year-olds.

Tasks

- Use the **My action planning sheet** to help you plan your work.

- **Collect** some toothpaste advertisements from newspapers and magazines. If possible record some television advertisements.

- **Share** your collection of advertisements with others in your group. **Discuss** how they present information and ideas about toothpaste. How do they present these ideas? How effective do you consider the advertisements to be? Use the **Discussion sheet** to note down your comments.

- Using the information you have gathered, **plan and design** your own toothpaste advertisement that you think would appeal to seven-year-olds. Use the **Advertisement guide** to help you.

- **Write** a point of view about your advertisement justifying why you think your advertisement will work! Use the **My point of view guide** to help you.

Extension work

- Design a toothpaste tube and packaging for your toothpaste.
- Plan and perform a television advertisement for your toothpaste.

Planning guidelines

What to do:

1. Read the task sheets carefully then make up your action plan of tasks to do and when to do them by completing the 'My action planning sheet'. Ask your teacher to help you with anything you are not sure of.

2. When looking at the collection of toothpastes and packaging, make a special note of what attracts your attention the most. What stands out? Why? What would make you want to pick this brand off the supermarket shelf rather than another brand?

3. Ask your teacher's help if you are having trouble finding out the meaning of some of the special terms and ingredients.

4. Use the 'Resources' sheet to help you find places to look for information about the function and care of teeth. A visit to a dentist would be very helpful! Remember to ask your teacher's permission before contacting anyone or using the internet.

5. When you are planning your talk to the seven-years-olds, remember to make it suitable and interesting enough for their age level. Young children like to look at pictures so make sure you have plenty of things for them to look at. Don't make the talk too long or they will lose interest.

6. When discussing the collection of toothpaste advertisements, try and work out what it is that makes one advertisement better than another. How important are scientific facts? Would some advertisements appeal more to adults than to children? What do you think would most interest a seven-year-old in using toothpaste? How will you make it seem like a good idea?

7. Think very carefully about the design of your advertisement. How much writing will you use? What colours do you think will be most effective? What pictures will you use? Use the advertisement guide to help you.

8. When writing your point of view remember that you are trying to help people understand your advertisement better. Explain why you have done certain things in your design and why you think your advertisements will appeal to seven-year-olds.

Resources

Teeth and toothpaste

Internet	About teeth *www.learn.co.uk/default.asp?WCI=SubUnit&WCU=9391* *www.bupa.co.uk/health_information/asp/healthy_living/dental_health/* Advertisement *www.healthyteeth.org*	Try CD-Rom encyclopaedias
Speakers and other sources	A dentist could tell you about what toothpaste is made of and about the function of teeth. Toothpaste companies will have publicity information you could send for. A school nurse could also give you information about how to care for your teeth. A local advertiser could talk to you about advertisements.	Contact by writing or phoning – ask your teacher first.
Libraries	The library will have reference books on teeth, dictionaries for meanings and books on advertising.	The librarian will help you.
Visits	When you visit your dentist tell them about your work, they may be able to help with information. A local newspaper may show you round its marketing and advertising department.	These can be individual or group visits. Discuss places to visit with friends.
Audience	Your group, teacher, visitors and seven-year-olds.	
Your own ideas	Discuss your ideas with your friends, your group and teacher. Visitors may give you feedback about your ideas.	Discuss your ideas with friends and your teacher.

Presentation guide

Teeth and toothpaste

My presentation

A presentation

A presentation is an illustrated talk presenting information to an audience.

You are going to plan and give a presentation aimed at seven-year-olds to tell them about how using toothpaste can keep their teeth healthy.

Remember

Make sure you have included all the necessary information.

Practice presenting your talk.

Use pictures to liven up your talk.

Try to make your talk interesting enough for seven-year-olds.

Things to think about

Decide what facts you wish to use. List them.
How will you begin your presentation?
What information do you need to provide?
How will you make sure the talk is suitable for children aged seven?
How will you make your talk interesting?
What pictures will you use?
How long will the talk be?
What do you want the children to learn?

Introduction

How will you begin your talk?

You will need to tell them who you are and what the talk will be about.

Development

Remember to explain what teeth are and why it is so important that we care for them.

Tell the children how they can care for their teeth properly.

Explain what toothpaste is and what we should use it for.

Conclusion

Remind the children that good care of their teeth is important.

Explain how a dentist can help them care for their teeth.

Discussion sheet

Read and compare a selection of toothpaste advertisements.
Make notes about the following things:

What **facts** are given about toothpaste?
List them.

What **opinions** are given about toothpaste? List them.

What words are used to persuade you that toothpaste will keep your teeth healthy? List them.

How is colour used? What effects do you think some colours will have on the reader?

What effect do you think the layout has on the reader? Explain how the following may encourage the reader to buy the toothpaste:

pictures

tables/charts with facts in them

the use of bullet points

the use of a logo

any other points you notice

140 **Literacy**
Challenges

Remember

Make sure you have included all the necessary information.

You have to make your toothpaste sound better than all the rest!

You need to explain how the toothpaste keeps teeth healthy.

Your target audience is children who are only seven.

Advertisement

An advertisement is a public announcement designed with the purpose of informing and/or changing the public's attitude or behaviour or getting them to buy a product.

You are going to design a toothpaste advertisement that will appeal to seven-year-olds.

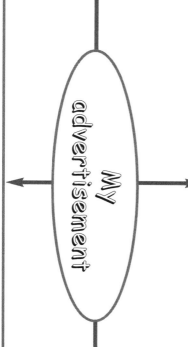

My advertisement

Things to think about

What do you want the reader to learn from this advertisement?
How will the reader know what you mean?
What facts and opinions will you use?
What persuasive words will you use?
What pictures/illustrations will be included?
How will you use colours in the advertisement?
Will you use different styles and sizes of text?
Are you going to design a special logo?
How will you make it appeal to seven-year-olds?

Planning

When you are designing your advert, you need to think about the following things:

What kind of advert will it be?
Will it have pictures and words?
Will it be handmade or computer generated?

What name will you give your toothpaste?
How can you use this name effectively in the advertisement?

Why do you want to sell this product?
Do you want seven-year-olds to have healthy teeth?
Do you want to earn a living selling toothpaste?

My point of view

Teeth and toothpaste

Point of view

A point of view is what you think about something. It is your opinion.

You are going to write a point of view about your completed toothpaste advertisement, saying why you think your advertisement is effective.

Remember

Check that you have explained why you used particular words and pictures.

Make sure you convince the readers to buy your toothpaste!

Check your spelling and punctuation.

Things to think about

How did you choose the name for your toothpaste? What is special about the sound of it? Is it easy to remember?

Why did you design your advert as you did?

Did you choose colours and fonts specially to create certain effects?

Did you invent a logo? How effective do you think it is?

Why do you think people will be tempted to try your toothpaste after reading your advertisement?

My advertisement

Introduction

Say what your advert is about.

Say why you called your toothpaste by its name.

Say who the advert is aimed at.

Development

Explain the layout of your advertisement. Why did you do it in that particular way.

Say how you have used colours and writing styles to create different effects.

Give examples of persuasive words used and say how these would influence the reader to buy the product.

Conclusion

Explain why your advert will appeal to seven-year-olds and why you think they would buy your toothpaste.

Challenge sheet

The challenge:

Name: _____

Start date: _____

Completion date: _____

My comments about the completed task:

Teacher's comments:

My action planning sheet

Date to start task	Task to be carried out and by whom	Date to complete task

Skills sheet – 1

Name: _____ Date: _____

	I can do this	I need more help to do this
Speaking and Listening – I can:		
• talk using words which help people to understand my ideas.		
• say what I think about a topic.		
• take turns in discussions with others.		
• explain my ideas and views.		
• summarise points in discussion.		
• develop my ideas with thought and in detail.		
• use good English in my presentations.		
• present my ideas to different audiences.		
• explore in talk the different ideas and features in advertisements.		
• ask questions which help me to understand the topic better.		
• talk well in my group.		
Reading – I can:		
• read and understand important ideas.		
• read different texts to find out their meaning.		
• read about different characters and explain what they are like.		
• identify subject words in my reading.		
• read fluently and understand what I am reading.		
• select information from different types of texts.		
• identify facts and opinions.		
• read and use difficult texts in my work.		
Writing:		
• My writing is clear and joined and can be read easily.		
• I use punctuation correctly in my writing.		
• I can check my writing and edit it.		
• I can plan different types of writing.		
• My writing shows that I understand what I read.		
• I can write using notes to explain what I have read.		

Skills sheet – 2

Name: _____   Date: _____

	I can do this	I need more help to do this
• I can set out my work in different ways:		
– in a letter		
– in a brochure		
– in a newspaper		
– in a display		
• I can write using words that are persuasive.		
• I can present my point of view in my writing.		
History – I can:		
• find out about events and people using books and other information sources.		
• ask and answer questions about history events.		
• write about my knowledge of history in different ways.		
• research for information and make notes on what I have read.		
Geography – I can:		
• ask and find the answers to questions about geography.		
• use different sources of information.		
• identify places and say what they are like.		
• explain how places are similar		
• explain how places are different.		
Science – I can:		
• investigate different sources of information to find answers to questions in a text.		
• use my observations to draw conclusions.		
• use my observations to evaluate information.		
• understand how electricity is used.		
• explain the part science has played in the development of useful inventions.		
• show that I understand what teeth are and how to care for them.		

Name: _____ Date: _____

	I can do this	I need more help to do this
Music – I can:		
• explain how different times in history can influence the sort of music that is composed.		
• explain how the place the composer is in can influence the sort of music created.		
Art and Design – I can:		
• use different starting points		
– pictures		
– stories		
– playscripts		
– fiction and non-fiction texts		
to plan my work.		
• use different materials to make:		
– a model		
– a poster		
– a picture		
– a collage		
• collect visual information (pictures) to plan the setting of my play		
• analyse my work		
• discuss the work of different artists and say what I like or dislike about their work.		
PE – I can:		
• prepare for exercise safely.		
• explain how exercise affects my body.		
• explain why doing physical activity is good for my health.		
Design and Technology – I can:		
• investigate products and think about how they work.		
• work out how products can be used.		
• find out what people think about the products they use.		

Skills sheet – 4

Name: _____ Date: _____

	Achieved	To achieve
• explain my design ideas clearly.		
• inform about my ideas through		
– discussion		
– drawing		
– models		
• evaluate my work.		
• identify what I need to do to improve my work.		
ICT – I can:		
• use ICT to present information in different ways:		
– playscripts		
– brochures		
– newspapers		
– advertisements		
• use ICT to change the presentation of my work.		
• communicate information using ICT which is suitable for my audience.		
• use ICT to research for information I need.		
• use different programs to complete the tasks I am set.		
PHSE – I can:		
• explain what a healthy lifestyle is.		
• explain my views to others.		
• understand that I have responsibilities to my school community.		
• write about my opinions.		
• discuss my views.		
• explain why bullying, lying and stealing can hurt others.		
• show that I understand why rules are needed.		
• explain how rules are made.		